Sensitive

Tanja Bulatovic

Copyright © 2019 Tanja Bulatovic
All Rights Reserved

DEDICATION

This book is dedicated with all my heart to those suffering with Electromagnetic Hypersensitivity and/or other chronic 'mystery illnesses' such as Multiple Chemical Sensitivity Syndrome, Chronic Fatigue Syndrome, Fibromyalgia, Post Traumatic Stress Disorder, Multiple Sclerosis and more.

DISCLAIMER

The author of this book is not a doctor or healthcare professional. The material in this book is not intended as a substitute for trained medical or psychological advice. Readers are advised to consult their licensed healthcare professional for any medical advice to treat any illness or symptoms. The intent of the author is only to offer information of a general nature to help you in your quest for emotional and spiritual well-being. The author expressly disclaims any liability for injuries resulting from use by readers of the methods contained herein.

ACKNOWLEDGMENTS

Merci Fabrice, for believing I was sick when doctors said I was nuts. I never would have survived without your love, your heartfelt, massive, daily hugs and foot rubs and everything else you did to help on a daily basis. You are the best! Even better than cheese! Je t'aime.

Thank you Keely for being a kindred-spirit-angel, who understands that sometimes things just fall apart. In a way, I think of you as a soul sister and I'm ever so grateful for your friendship and support, on the good and bad days.

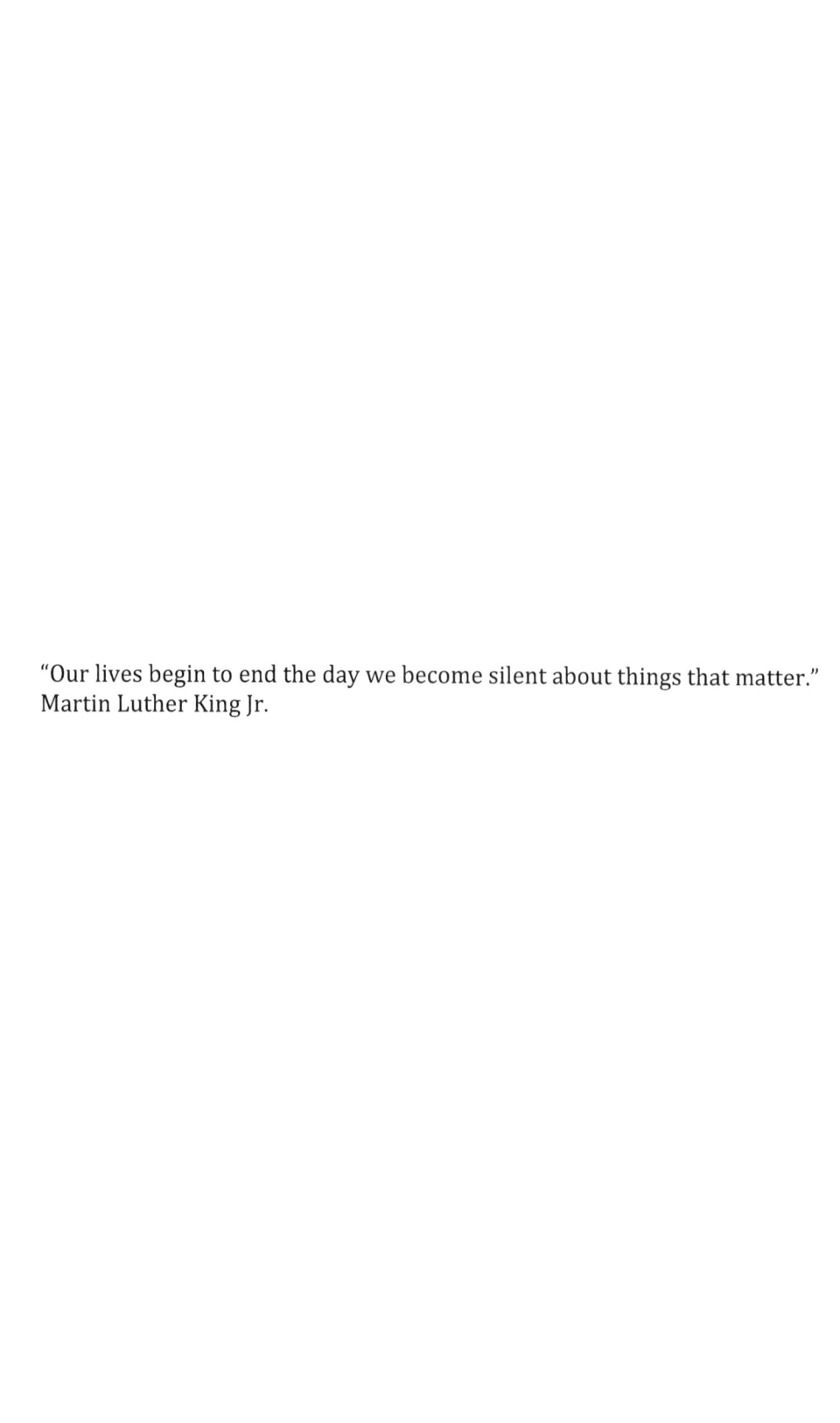

"Our lives begin to end the day we become silent about things that matter."
Martin Luther King Jr.

TABLE OF CONTENTS

Introduction
Is this Book for You?
This Book May Not be of Interest to You...
How is this Book Structured?
Part 1- Understanding EHS
What is EHS?
Common EHS Symptoms
How Many People are affected?
Why Nobody Gets It
Scientific Research
Who is WHO?
Proof and Denial
Cell Phone Dangers
Cell Phones and Breast Cancer
The Hazard of Living Near Cell Towers
Conflicting Information
Proving the Lie
Anecdotal Evidence
The Increased Risk to Children
The Risk to Animals
The Risk to the Environment
Part 2: How to Diagnose and Treat EHS
My Journey
Emotional and Social Impact of EHS
Key Symptoms to Look for
Common Secondary Symptoms
Finding the Right Doctor
Finally an Official Diagnosis
How EHS is Diagnosed
Part 3: Self-Help for Electro-Sensitive People
What are the Treatment Options?
First Aid Protection from EMF Pollution
Foods to Fortify the Body
Helpful Supplements
Life-Style Practices
Conclusion
Final Thoughts
Health Resources
About the Author

Introduction

Welcome and thanks for choosing 'Sensitive'.
This tiny book took five years to write. The pages within it contain the sum of my EHS journey. A journey I needed to write, to plant a seed in the garden of your mind. With the hope it may be of interest to those who find themselves in a similar position to me, or, those looking for a better understanding of what Electromagnetic Hypersensitivity Syndrome (EHS) is.

I feel what is missing out there is an understanding of the EMF Crisis. An understanding of what EHS people are living on a daily basis. And what to expect from an emotional and physical point of view. As well as how to move forward by nourishing your mind, body and spirit. That's my attempt here with this book.

Sounds strange, but in retrospect, I believe I needed to become EHS to fulfill my larger purpose, which is to be of some help to humanity. Yet, for the past few years I was shy of my calling and used my illness to hide from the world (and from myself), while seeking the approval of those around me by pretending that nothing was wrong.

I wanted to be like everyone else, to fit in. In doing so, I made my life even more challenging and difficult. It has taken a while, but now I recognize EHS as a gift, and a blessing, by which I can achieve what I was assigned to accomplish. Being EHS may be one of the hardest things I've had to go through, but it is also one of the truest. When we are true to ourselves, in spite of our circumstances, it helps the whole world.

Today, this Australian expat actor/writer is proud to call herself an Electromagnetic Hypersensitive person. I wasn't always so proud, of course. When I got sick I was terrified, lost, misunderstood, and bullied by certain people and 'friends'. I wondered what the hell was wrong with me…? Why was I lumbered with this sensitivity? And most of all, why wasn't *everybody* sensitive to Electromagnetic Frequencies… why me? Over all, I liked to think of myself as an intuitive, empathic, sensitive being… but THIS?

You see, I'd never questioned Electromagnetic pollution. Hadn't paid any attention. Couldn't care less about it! Can you relate? What I'm saying is this: If I never bothered to question man-made Electromagnetic Frequencies and all these gadgets we take for granted, maybe you haven't either.

I loved technology as much as the next person. I loved the Internet and the freedom it provides. In fact, I used to pride myself on being a digital nomad. On being able to work on my laptop while sitting under a coconut tree on some tropical beach paradise. 'Location independence', and 'perpetual travel' became my mottos. Like most people my age, I'd used a mobile phone for 20+ years and a cordless phone at home. I would get annoyed about a shitty reception, or the lack of cell towers without giving it a second's thought. Who knew, back then, that being fried by man-made Electromagnetic Radiation was dangerous???

Now. I've been posting on the dangers of EMF's (and recently 5G) for years... and I noticed that clearly, not many people are all that interested. So why bother with the canary in the coalmine act... I hear you ask. Well, here's why:

Because... even if I get to help just one person, it'll be worth the effort.

And because silence is far worse. When people stay silent, bad things happen.

Which brings us to the topic at hand.

Electromagnetic Frequencies (EMF's). You can't see them. You can't feel them. That is, unless you have EHS. Such is the case, for 3% of the world's population (as of writing) and numbers are on the rise. In fact, most people, unless they measure the EMF fields around them, are clueless as to the intensity of EMF exposures we have.

We are only beginning to understand that Electromagnetic Hypersensitivity Syndrome (EHS) is a multisystemic condition in response to even weak electromagnetic fields. And we're only beginning to understand that EMF's affect us at a cellular level. In fact, EMF's affect all of us all of the time. As I said, we don't know it because we can't see them and most of us (as yet) can't feel them. And we think if we can't see them, they're not there, right?

By the same token, we are currently witnessing the greatest public health disaster in human history. Despite serious health concerns, devices that emit EMF radiation, including Wi-Fi routers, wireless computers, security systems, Bluetooth, smart meters, mobile phones and now, wearable computer watches, have become commonplace.
Cancer, infertility, ADHD, headaches and cognitive problems are just some of the health risks linked to Electromagnetic Radiation. Today, a growing number of people are experiencing symptoms linked to electronic devices.

The industry, however, seems immune to this. They are simply going ahead without our permission, while 200 000 medical doctors and scientists are worried. But this is ignored, and nobody will do a thing about it.

"Electromagnetic (EMF) pollution may be the most significant form of pollution human activity has produced in this century, all the more dangerous because it is invisible and insensible." Dr. Andrew Weil, M.D., Natural Health Expert

IS THIS BOOK FOR YOU?

Ever noticed that you feel a little strange after using a mobile phone, Wi-Fi, hands-free etc.? If your answer is yes, pay attention, because it means you are mildly EHS. If so, you need to educate yourself before things get worse. Before you are forced to live as a recluse in the forest or in a cave somewhere. I'm not kidding.

This is already happening all over the world. And it's happening to people from all walks of life (more about that later).
Thing is, as long as you still have a choice in the matter you can do something about it. You can gain the knowledge to keep safe.

A good part of my reason for being in this life is to make sense, from a holistic perspective of this sensitivity, not only to understand it but also to turn it around and see it as a positive thing. For example, my body senses EMF's. It certainly doesn't like them. But I believe I'm one of the lucky ones. At least I know what's going on now, so I can protect and strengthen my body/mind/spirit and help others do the same.
Therefore, this book documents parts of my personal journey towards a diagnosis as being EHS, the ensuing questions it raised, along with information, which might assist fellow sufferers to better cope with this frightening condition.

Unfortunately to most people, EHS and the dangers of EMF's are still unknown or unheard of. Perhaps you've read or seen something related to EHS, but shrugged it off thinking it doesn't concern you, or that it's a weird illness that affects only those who are 'hypersensitive' to microwave radiation.

Your reaction would be perfectly normal. I mean, most people are more concerned about the state of the economy or the football results than questioning the health effects of man-made Electromagnetic Frequencies. I was one of those people. But via my own diagnoses, I've learned a lot along the way.

THIS BOOK MAY NOT BE OF INTEREST TO YOU...

If you don't believe EHS exists regardless of a tons of scientific evidence clearly stating it does (read the BioInitiative Report). https://bioinitiative.org/
If you believe it's normal to be over-exposed to man-made electromagnetic waves.
If you believe that this deliberate 'cooking of humanity' doesn't affect you or the health of your kids.
If you believe that telecommunications companies and politicians have your best interests at heart.
You think you are six foot tall and bullet proof, EHS will never happen to YOU!
You'd rather be fried like a crispy Thai prawn as long as you stay 'connected' and couldn't give a damn about your health, let alone anybody else's.
If the above applies to you, by all means, don't bother reading. Having said that, people who don't know and/or don't get it, are exactly the ones who should read the book. Just saying...

HOW IS THIS BOOK STRUCTURED?

In Part 1 - Understanding EHS, I explain exactly the dangers of EMF's, what EHS is and why it is the emerging health problem of the 21st century – a serious environmental health issue that begs for our immediate attention. You will learn that it doesn't matter whether you've been diagnosed with EHS or not, as Electromagnetic Radiation affects every single human being, our environment and every animal species on this planet today.

In Part 2 - How to Diagnose and Treat EHS, I share how EHS has affected my life on a personal level. I also talk about the symptoms and the diagnosis. Even if you aren't suffering from a debilitating 'mystery illness' like EHS, MCS, Chronic Fatigue, Fibromyalgia, you'll be amazed at how many symptoms you can relate to. And how much better you will feel once you incorporate a few simple changes into your daily life. Sufferers will realize they are not crazy. They are not imagining their symptoms. And they are definitely not alone.

Part 3 – Self-Help for Electro-Sensitive People introduces some First Aid methods of self-protection by means of shielding your immediate environment, and looking after your body with healing foods, supplements and life-style choices. You will learn that even though living in this overly zapped world is a 24/7 problem, there is hope. I've spent years accumulating this information at a time when there was little help available for people like me. Out of sheer desperation I also spent a small fortune on supposed EMF protection gadgets people are trying to cash in on (probably the same people who made us sick in the first place).

Today, as a result, I'm in a pretty good position to help you discern what you need and don't need to spend your hard-earned money on. Most of the gadgets won't do the job. But there are some simple measures you can take to strengthen your body and immune system, so you can get back on track and lead an almost normal life. Trust me, an almost normal life beats the hell out of spending most of your time bedridden because your body can't function anymore. I know how that feels. And I also know that I've been assigned this mountain to show others it can be moved.

It all begins with awareness. So prepare yourself for a huge learning curve. And get ready to take control of your own safety and healing. By taking some simple precautions, I sincerely hope you can stay safe in the Digital Age. There's really no time to waste.

Shall we get started?

"For the first time in our evolutionary history, we have generated an entire secondary, virtual, densely complex environment—an electromagnetic soup—that essentially overlaps the human nervous system,"- Michael Persinger, PhD, a neuroscientist at Laurentian University who has studied the effects of EMFs on cancer cells

PART 1 – UNDERSTANDING ELECTRO-SENSITIVITY (EHS)

WHAT IS EHS?

"Electromagnetic hypersensitivity is characterized by an awareness and/or adverse symptomatology in response to even extremely weak electromagnetic fields of multiple types."– Doctor Erica Mallery Blythe

EHS is a physiological condition that presents with a variety of neurological and immunological symptoms. These symptoms intensify with exposure to electric and magnetic fields, like those emitted by computers, Wi-Fi, mobile phones, power lines, and everyday appliances like your refrigerator. And they get worse the longer you're exposed to electric and magnetic fields or any type of electromagnetic radiation. Symptoms and their severity vary from person to person. Depending on how much EMF you're exposing yourself to.

As an aside: There are 64 million mobile phones in France for 60 million French people, with around 300 000 cell towers in frequencies of GSM, UMTS, 3G, 4G, and (as of writing) soon-to-be 5G. In mid 2014, there were more active SIM cards/mobile phones on the planet than humans.

"If EHS is unmanaged and there is general deterioration, there will be reaction to an increasingly broad range of frequencies at increasingly low intensities, i.e. the number of devices complained of triggering symptoms will increase and symptomatic distances will decrease", - Dr. Erica Mallery-Blythe.

The above statement by Dr Erica Mallery-Blythe means that EHS is cumulative. Meaning your body develops more serious issues over time. And you may find you become more and more sensitive as time goes by. Long days at the laptop that may have once caused a mild headache can become 10 minutes at the laptop that results in an excruciating migraine and a bunch of other unpleasant symptoms that take a week or more to recover from.

Sufferers experience a variety of symptoms whenever they are near EMF pollution. Symptoms generally dissipate as they remove themselves from the source of the pollution. For some people, that may mean taking regular breaks from their laptops. For others, myself included, this means a total disruption of their lives. An inability to tolerate any EMF pollution, resulting in relocating to EMF-free rural areas (almost impossible as there are few) and an inability even to venture out to the local grocery store.

John J. O'Neill (1968) wrote the following in his Pulitzer-prize-winning biography of Nicola Tesla (one of the first EHS sufferers). Here he describes Tesla's illness, which looked very much like an environmental hypersensitivity disorder:

"The peculiar malady that now affected him was never diagnosed by the doctors who attended him. It was, however, an experience that nearly cost him his life. To doctors he appeared to be at death's door. The strange manifestations he exhibited attracted the attention of a renowned physician, who declared that medical science could do nothing to aid him. One of the symptoms of the illness was an acute sensitivity of all the sense organs. His senses had always been extremely keen, but this sensitivity was now so tremendously exaggerated that the effects were a form of torture. The ticking of watch three rooms away sounded like the beat of hammers on an anvil. The vibration of ordinary city traffic, when transmitted through a chair or bench, pounded through his body. It was necessary to place the legs of his bed on rubber pads to eliminate the vibrations. Ordinary speech sounded like thunderous pandemonium. The slightest touch had the mental effect of a tremendous blow. A beam of sunlight shining on him produced the effect of an internal explosion. In the dark he could sense an object at a distance of a dozen feet by a peculiar creepy sensation in his forehead. His whole body was constantly wracked by twitches and tremors. His pulse, he said, would vary from a few feeble throbs per minute to more than one hundred and fifty. Throughout this mysterious illness he was fighting with a powerful desire to recover his normal condition. He had before him a task he must accomplish – he must attain the solution of the alternating-current motor problem."

To be clear, Electromagnetic Hypersensitivity (EHS) is nothing new. This physiological condition has existed since 1932. That said, you would think that more of the world would be aware of the dangers by now. You would think that every country would have invested significant resources into combatting this condition. Also known as EMF Intolerance Syndrome, Rapid Aging Syndrome, Microwave Sickness, and Radio Wave Syndrome, whatever you want to call it, the condition is real. All of us, in fact all living things are electro-sensitive to some degree. Even if you don't feel any obvious effects and develop severe and debilitating EHS, your biology is still affected because any unnatural exposure to EMF's stresses the body. Why? Our bodies are not made to withstand the constant exposure that has become the norm in the Digital Age.

"Sensitivity to electromagnetic radiation is the emerging health problem of the 21st century. It is imperative health practitioners, governments, schools and parents learn more about it. The human health stakes are significant". William Rea, MD

COMMON EHS SYMPTOMS

Let's look at some of the symptoms associated with EHS. Remember, everyone reacts in a different way to EMF exposure and will experience a differing set of symptoms. Some will experience a dizzying array of debilitating symptoms. They can include headaches, chronic fatigue, fainting, light and noise sensitivity, heart problems, and many, many more, which I'll cover later.

Others will only experience minor ones they may dismiss as normal. Aside from the overwhelming list of possible adverse health effects, it's also important to note that many people suffer a loss of homeostasis and a general loss of well-being. It's also likely that you'll accumulate more symptoms as time passes or notice that your current symptoms get worse. Remember, just because you don't have debilitating symptoms, does not mean you're not sensitive to EMF's.

The term 'Electromagnetic Hypersensitivity' is a name given to people like me, who are seriously affected and have bodies that don't like living in the modern world. Symptoms range from mild to debilitating. As mentioned, it is a progressive illness. It can get worse. Don't think you are only mildly affected, and feel that you're ok without protecting yourself. That's the worst thing you can do. The mild symptoms can quickly grow and turn you into a barely functioning being. As mentioned above, symptoms are accumulative and are in direct proportion to how clean or polluted your environment is. Here's a quick list of common symptoms:

Abdominal pain
Altered reflexes
Anger
Arrhythmias
Asthma
Auditory disturbances (especially Tinnitus)
Blood sugar problems
Blurred vision
Bronchitis
Burning skin (like sunburn)
Chronic Fatigue
Depression
Deteriorating vision
Difficulty concentrating
Difficulty with memory
Digestive problems
Dizziness
Dreamless sleep
Dry skin
Enlarged thyroid
Facial flushing
Fever
Flu-like symptoms
Frequent urination
General pain and discomfort
Hair loss
Headaches (ranging from mild to blinding)
High blood pressure
Histamine Intolerance
Hyperactivity
Hypoglycemia
Hypoxia
Impaired sense of smell
Incontinence

Increased allergies
Increased thirst
Insomnia
Internal bleeding
Irritability
Itching
Joint pain
Leg/foot pain
Light sleep
Light-headedness
Loss of balance
Low blood pressure
Membrane Sensitivity
Mood swings
Muscle pain
Muscle Spasms
Muscle Twitching
Nausea
Night sweats
Nosebleeds
Numbness
Palpitations
Parasthesia
PMS
Pneumonia
Pressure in chest
Prone to infections
Rapid heart rate
Restless Leg Syndrome
Ringing in the ears
Sensory up-regulation
Shortness of breath
Sinusitis
Skin rash
Sleep disturbances
Sleeping too much (my case)
Slow heart rate/ Fast heart rate
Swollen lymph nodes
Temper tantrums
Tingling and buzzing in hands, legs, feet
Tooth pain
Tremors
Un-restful sleep
Unusual pain at multiple sites
Visual disturbances
Weakened immune system
Weakness
Weight loss/ Inability to lose weight

HOW MANY PEOPLE ARE AFFECTED?

This is a difficult one to quantify. Many people are unaware of the fact that they are suffering. In reality, EHS affects 100% of the population. That's right. Even at low levels, every living cell suffers a negative biological impact from exposure to EMF's. Even if you don't realize it, and have no ill effects, this Digital Age in which we live is harming you. And your baby. And your beloved dog. And your child's hamster. And your favorite pot plant.

EMF's affect millions of people across the globe. Although they don't realize that EMF pollution is the cause of their mystery symptoms. Electromagnetic Hypersensitivity Syndrome affects around 20 to 25% of the world's population. At the time of writing, 3 to 5% are moderately affected and 1% is severely affected. And numbers are on the increase.

EMF pollution is in our homes, workplaces, entertainment venues, and pretty much everywhere else. When Dr Belpomme diagnosed me in Paris-France in 2014, 6000 people had a positive diagnosis. By 2016, there were 12 0000 diagnosed cases in France. This doesn't account for the 1000's of people with 'mystery symptoms' who've had no diagnosis and have no idea.

Funny enough, Sweden acknowledges EHS as an impairment, where it isn't a taboo illness. At the time of writing, around 300 000 people in Sweden are afflicted with EHS. And figures are expected to get worse, unless we all take steps to protect ourselves.

Remember that some people don't connect their symptoms with EHS. So many people dismiss their symptoms as 'normal' or just as general poor health.

"The U.S. spends over $2 trillion dollars on health care each year, of which about 78% is from people with chronic illnesses, without adequately exploring and understanding what factors—including EMF/RF—contribute to imbalances in peoples' bodies' in the first place. After reading The BioInitiative Report, it should come as no surprise to policymakers, given the continually increasing levels of EMF/RF exposures in our environment, that close to 50% of Americans now live with a chronic illness. I grieve for people who needlessly suffer these illnesses and hold out the hope that our government leaders will become more cognizant of the role electromagnetic factors are playing in disease, health care costs and the erosion of quality of life and productivity in America."
Camilla Rees, MBA, CEO, Wide Angle Health, LLC Patient education and advocacy

WHY NOBODY GETS IT

The answer is, on the surface at least, a simple one. Most people don't get EHS because they can't see it. It's a little bit like the dismissal and stigma that surrounds mental health conditions. People assume that you're making up your symptoms. Or imagining them because on the outside, you don't look like there's anything wrong. There's a struggle to grasp the concept. Or to develop an understanding of something one can't see. And, with EHS, the potential repercussions for other people, if your symptoms and your condition are real, are huge, so it's better and easier to dismiss you as a crazy person.

Government propaganda, their blatant denial of the dangers of electromagnetism, and their so-called "independent" studies that never find any conclusive evidence also ensure that the majority of the general public stay unaware. Oblivious to the danger around them
As all electric and wireless devices generate electromagnetism, if it were an officially recognized condition with more safeguards in place, it would amount to a huge economic cost. Never mind the cost of health compensation for damages inflicted on human beings.

Big corporations would be forced to ensure the smartphones, tablets, laptops, and every other electronic product was actually safe to use. Of course, their money concerns by far outweigh any health implications like cancer clusters, the debilitating effects of EMF on sensitive individuals, and the increased prevalence of devastating childhood cancers.

Instead, our governments deny the dangers. Just a second...isn't that what happened with cigarettes and asbestos too? Claiming that those of us who suffer from EHS or try to educate everyone on the dangers are nothing but kooks, conspiracy theorists and crackpots. They tell consumers not to worry. To just keep buying and using deadly devices like good little sheep. And don't think about the consequences.

And that, my friends, is why nobody gets it. Because EMF's are an invisible menace. Because the powers that be, do everything they can to keep people uninformed. And because money and business is more important than the health of every human, every animal, every plant and every single living organism, on our fragile planet.

SCIENTIFIC RESEARCH

A large part of the arguments against the reality of EHS and the risk EMF's pose to every living thing relates to the fact that, supposedly, the available data is only anecdotal. Or it does not follow a proper scientific method. Or that it is, in some other way flawed. But that's not the case. Yes, there is a lot of anecdotal evidence from across the globe – because there are many people suffering. And there are, most likely, many spurious supposed scientific studies. But there are also genuine independent scientific studies that provide irrefutable evidence and follow strict scientific protocols. Yet, they too, are dismissed as irrelevant.

Much of the research the naysayers are quoting as proof that EHS is a lie is from the mid 1990s. Remember those bricks that passed as mobile phones in those days? And had you ever heard of Wi-Fi, broadband, or Bluetooth? Did you have wireless gamepads for your PlayStation? Wireless headphones? Smart watches? Live streaming?

Technology has advanced by a staggering degree in the last 20 years. It is high time they bring the research as up to date as our technology. The published findings of those outdated studies are, inconclusive. The wording is clever, like with so many of these studies...

"There isn't enough evidence to support a finding of..." or "The available evidence does not provide irrefutable proof linking EMF's as the direct cause...".

Slowly but surely they are conducting more and more studies into the health effects of EMF's. And much of the old data is still relevant. You can, for example, see a report from the US Naval Medical Research Institute that lists an incredible 2300 studies detailing the biological impact of EMF's, up to 1971. While this particular document doesn't go into excessive detail, it acts as a bibliography or library of studies reporting biological phenomena and clinical manifestations attributed to microwave radio frequency radiation.

A $25 million study conducted in May 2016, by the US National Toxicology Program (NTP), showed a significant increase in the prevalence of cancer among rats exposed to EMF's. Specifically, they found the exposed rats had higher rates of two cancers. One, a glioma, is a type of brain tumor. The second, a Schwannoma, a rare tumor of the heart. Note that during this study, none of the rats in the control group developed either of these types of tumors.

You can find all sorts of scientific evidence. From a 1976 defence intelligence agency report, describing the physical symptoms of military personnel exposed to microwave radiation. To a 2015 study showing exposure to 2.4 GHz Wi-Fi decreases sperm function and motility. The sheer amount of research and number of papers is actually quite staggering. Yet despite the volume of convincing evidence, EHS is still dismissed as imaginary. And those trying to promote awareness (including many doctors) of the danger we all face are ridiculed, accused of fear-mongering, and sidelined by many of their peers.

Seemingly, however many studies are conducted, it's never enough. There are constant requests for further research or more evidence. Or the health, science, and government bodies to whom these findings are reported promise to investigate further, but it never seems to materialize. Why? Money talks. Scientific Research is funded by people who have a conflict of interest. (Scientists also have bills to pay). Companies are driven by profit (just like pharmaceutical companies).

Even though WHO (World Health Organization) have recognized EHS as a real condition, statistics are inaccurate. Why? Because 100% of people are cellularly affected. WHO classified mobiles as possible carcinogenic against humans. Ever actually read the small print in the brochure when you buy a mobile phone. No? Neither did I. If you do, you'll see (as previously discussed) that they issue a warning to never speak with the mobile pressed against your ear/head, but instead to keep it several inches away from the body. How many of us know that? Therein, an increased risk of brain tumors. And yes, the proof is there. Mobile phones cause brain tumors. Now, if they can damage the human brain, why not the entire being? So many people are exposed, we can no longer analyze as in exposed vs. people not exposed. All of us are exposed all the time.

Another point worth mentioning is this: they test phones on adult heads. What about children who have smaller, thinner heads with tiny brains not yet developed? Engineers who have no idea what goes on in a human cell do these tests. So it's clear. The change has to come from us, not them.

WHO IS WHO?

Researchers at the World Health Organization also known as WHO study anything and everything that could have a negative impact on the health of the world's population. Their findings are interesting – and, at times conflicting. They, along with the IARC, or International Agency for Research on Cancer, classified RF's (radio magnetic frequencies) as a Group 2b Possible Human Carcinogen in 2012. In spite of these findings, these organizations published little further conclusive research. And the information was not communicated to the population in many countries. You'd think these determinations would've given rise to extensive research to find conclusive answers. Instead, they made little evidential progress.

As Dr. Erica Mallery-Blythe points out, "Conversely, it (the classification of RF as a possible human carcinogen) was not even mentioned in the AGNIR government-commissioned paper a year later."

Much of the published findings from WHO, particularly those from the early days are double-edged. For example, their paper, EMF & Cancer: Epidemiologic Evidence to Date, by Dr. Leeka I Kheifets, states that the pooled analysis of two epidemiological studies into childhood leukemia "suggest that, in a population exposed to average magnetic fields in excess of 0.3 to 0.4 uT, twice as many children might develop leukemia compared to a population with lower exposures."

And while it should be noted that average or regular exposure to over 0.3 uT is not the norm, it does happen, and if the risk is magnified so much at that level, there is obviously a significant, if lower risk, at lower exposure. This same paper also found that the instances of adulthood leukemia and brain tumors were higher in electrical workers who were regularly exposed to EMF's.

Then, in their 2007 Electromagnetic Fields and Public Health backgrounder, or fact sheet, they claim that the evidence of the increased risk of childhood leukemia with exposure to EMR is not strong enough to be considered causal. And, if that weren't bad enough, the same paper says, based on the fact that childhood leukemia is comparatively rare, at 49,000 cases worldwide in 2000, "If ELF (extremely low frequency) magnetic fields actually do increase the risk of the disease [childhood leukemia], when considered in a global context, the impact on public health of ELF EMF exposure would be limited."

Any increase in childhood leukemia – or any other disease – is a significant impact on public health. Surely one of our primary goals is to ensure the next generation is strong and healthy? And any increased risk is a matter of real concern. As a parent, would you knowingly increase your child's risk of developing leukemia or a brain tumor?

On the plus side, the WHO now officially recognizes EHS as a condition. They even have a set of pages dedicated to EHS on their website and provide some fact sheets and papers devoted to the topic. One positive is that the WHO is finally taking EHS seriously. They are part of the International EMF project. This international project is intended to provide research and insight into growing concerns from the general public and health professionals across the globe regarding the health implications of increasingly high levels of exposure to low-level electromagnetic frequencies.

The WHO seem to understand this emerging and under researched area and one of the aims of this particular project is to identify where the gaps in the current knowledge are and where further research is needed. Part of their mission aims to encourage focused research programs in conjunction with funding agencies. They are aiming to compile the results of their research used in conjunction with WHO's environmental health criteria monographs. This lets them make detailed assessments on the risks posed by exposure to EMF. Based on these findings, the WHO will be able to help develop acceptable standards and guidelines to EMF exposure globally.

While the WHO are now trying to make inroads in the field of electromagnetic radiation effects on living organisms, there is still some criticism surrounding the organization. For example, there are those who believe former-WHO director, Gro Harlem Brundtland, was forced to resign after announcing that she suffers from EHS. The former Prime Minister of Norway, and former WHO director-general resigned less than a year after publicly announcing that she suffered from EHS, in what some believe to be mysterious circumstances. She claimed that she suffered whenever she used a mobile phone. "I never place a mobile phone next to my head because in one second I would develop a bad headache. I use the phone in speaker mode." Enough said.

PROOF AND DENIAL

"There is no question EMFs have a major effect on neurological functioning. They slow our brain waves and affect our long-term mental clarity. We should minimize exposures as much as possible to optimize neurotransmitter levels and prevent deterioration of health". - Eric Braverman, MD. (Brain researcher, Author of The Edge Effect, and Director of Path Medical in New York City and The PATH Foundation. Expert in the brain's global impact on illness and health.)

The real question we have to ask is why there isn't more concern over the horrifying effects and devastating long-term implications of Electromagnetic Radiation. Why isn't it all over the media? Why are no major news and scientific outlets making this stuff priority news? Why does the majority of governing bodies, corporations, pet scientists, and powerful companies deny that electromagnetic radiation is harmful? Why do so few of us know that EHS is a "thing"? This is the Digital Age. We're bombarded with information daily.

We find out about events, significant scientific research, celebrity drivel, and all the rest almost as soon as it happens, so why do so few of us know about EMFs and the dangers they pose? And, given that we've known about these dangers since the 1930s, why hasn't there been any real, significant research in this field? Why is it still classed as "emerging science" or "fringe science"?

Seeing they collected the first data in the 1930s, it's hardly an emerging field of science. Well, there is proof – overwhelming proof, in fact, but there are reasons for the crazy denial. Thankfully, some countries are waking up the dangers, at last, and making changes. But is it too little, too late?

As Doctor Mallery-Blythe points out, "EHS has been demonstrated in a published, peer-reviewed, double blind research study, as an 'environmentally inducible bona-fide neurological syndrome', and other provocation tests corroborate this evidence."

If that's the case, why won't more people and health bodies take it seriously?

CELL PHONE DANGERS

Let's dive in by taking a look at mobile phone 'small print'. Telecommunication companies and the governing bodies who make big bucks from said companies would have you believe there is no danger of any kind from exposure to the Wi-Fi signals and EMR their devices give off. No, you're not really sitting in a cloud of genotoxic electromagnetism every time you use your phone, or even have it switched on and within reach. It's perfectly safe. Just please, whatever you do, do not read the small print in the manual that comes with your phone.

You see, most people assume a cell phone is designed to be a handheld device. You are meant to hold it in your hand, and you are supposed to put it against your head when you don't want to talk on speakerphone, right? And, so, because that's what it is designed for, it must be safe for that purpose, right? And, if you can hold it in your hand to text, surf the web, play games, share stuff via your social channels, then it follows that it is perfectly safe to keep in your pocket, right? I mean, if there were serious risks associated with such behavior, surely there would be clear warning labels, like there are on cigarettes, right? Wrong on all counts, actually.

While all manufacturer guidance varies - because there is essentially no proper guidance from world governments, all manufacturers do, in fact, provide warnings and safe usage instructions in their documentation. However, it is either hidden - like in the Blackberry units, where the manual is on the phone itself, and you have to transverse five different steps within the phone settings to access the hidden warning - or it is included as a throwaway statement in the small print of the user manual.

Now yes, in theory, these companies are following the letter of the law, because they are including a warning consumers can access, providing they know where to look. But they aren't really following the spirit of the law, are they? These greedy giants know full well the risks their devices present, and instead of trying to make them safer, they simply sell you a potentially lethal device with a tiny, hidden warning, in full knowledge of the fact they've just sold you a device that could do you harm. And if there are any repercussions - well, they did provide a warning, didn't they? It's not their fault that you didn't thoroughly read every scrap of documentation. How were they to know you were going to hold the phone while it was turned on, or put it to your ear to talk to someone? They simply could not have predicted such behavior and they did everything they were legally obliged to do to keep you safe.

But dig deeper and look closely at the small print. You are warned to keep your phone a minimum distance (some manufacturers recommend as much as 30 centimeters) from your body while it is turned on - and further still if it is connected to a wireless network. You are told not to put the phone near your head or against any other part of your body because of the dangers of exposure to non ionizing radiation. Sneaky. And kind of terrifying. How many people routinely carry their phones in their pockets? How many people hold their cell phones against their heads while they chat to family and friends? A study conducted by the California Brain Tumor Association reported that 70% of adults in Berkeley did not know about the Federal Communication Commission's regulation that specifies the minimum separation distance from RF-emitting devices. And further, that 82% of respondents would like more information.

Ellen Marks, the executive director of the California Brain Tumor Association, says that although most cell phone manufacturers do include safety information, they make it very hard to find. She notes "BlackBerry manuals tell users to 'Keep the device at least 25mm from your body when the BlackBerry device is turned on and connected to a wireless network', but it takes five steps to find the warning." Here's the process:

1. Click on settings.
2. Go to "general".
3. Click on "About".
4. Find the "Legal" selection.
5. Hit "RF Exposure".

She also points out that most users don't know this information exists. Marks says "The public deserves the right to know that there is a safe distance information required by the FCC hidden deep in the phone or in the manual."

In light of undeniable proof and continued research, more countries and states are attempting to enforce "Right to Know" laws that require cellphone manufacturers to print clear warnings on the outside of cell phone packaging, like those you see on cigarettes and rolling tobacco. But the problem is that the cell phone and wireless companies are less than impressed with this - and they have major influence.

In San Francisco, for example, back in 2010, they approved regulations that forced cell phone companies to clearly display the Specific Absorption Rate, or SAR, (which is the amount of radio frequency energy absorbed by the body on the packaging of each individual cell phone). Sounds great, doesn't it? A real step forward. As soon as they approved this regulation, the Cellular Telephone Industries Association sued the city. They claimed that displaying these numbers would simply confuse consumers, rather than informing them - because, of course, we're all stupid. Because the data would imply that the lower the radiation levels, the safer the device, which wouldn't always be the clear-cut truth. The city backed down against the might of the communications giant and threw out the ordinance.

CELL PHONES AND BREAST CANCER

Over the past few years it seems that more women are storing their cell phones in their bras, presumably for convenience. Apparently, we store all kinds of things in our bras, including cell phones, hand sanitizer, money, and baby pacifiers.
This is another area that requires extensive research. Right now science cannot confirm or repudiate the claims made by many women and health professionals that wearing your cell phone in your bra or in the breast pocket of your shirt can cause you to develop breast cancer.

The current available evidence is inconclusive. While the increasing number of women, particularly younger women (under 30, and in some cases under 20), who develop breast cancer and who happen to carry their smartphones in their bras continues to rise, scientists cannot find a direct causal link or mechanism that would result in EMR causing specific types of cancer. It is interesting to note that often, the location of the tumor is on the same side and near to where they carry the phone.

In February 2015, they conducted a study, entitled 'Investigation of the effects of distance from sources on apoptosis, oxidative stress and cytosolic calcium accumulation via TRPV1 channels induced by mobile phones and Wi-Fi in breast cancer cells', by Bilal Çiğ,Mustafa Nazıroğlu, which appeared in 'Biochimica et Biophysica Acta (BBA) - Biomembranes' in October 2015, and provided conclusive evidence that the closer the RF exposure was to the skin of the test subjects, the more damage it caused the cells beneath.

The study found that this type of manmade radiation increased or generated reactive oxygen species, or ROS. This, in turn, disrupts the antioxidant mechanisms of the body, which increases oxidative stress and apoptosis, and, impairs the natural cell repair mechanisms within the body. The increased oxidation and reduced efficacy of cell repair can play a significant role in the development of cancer.

THE HAZARD OF LIVING NEAR CELL TOWERS

"The evidence for risks from prolonged cell phone and cordless phone use is quite strong when you look at people who have used these devices for 10 years or longer, and when they are used mainly on one side of the head. Recent studies thcat do not report increased risk of brain tumors and acoustic neuromas have not looked at heavy users, use over ten years or longer, and do not look at the part of the brain which would reasonably have exposure to produce a tumor." - Lennart Hardell, MD, PhD. Professor at University Hospital, Orebro, Sweden. World-renowned expert on cell phones, cordless phones, brain tumors, and the safety of wireless radiofrequency and microwave radiation. Co-authored the BioInitiative Report's section on Brain Tumors by Dr. Hardell

There's a lot of controversy surrounding mobile phone towers and whether living near one causes an increased risk of cancer. Many people claim that those who raise concerns over the health risks of cell phone towers are alarmists and fear-mongers, however, there is a large ever-growing body of evidence to suggest that proximity to mobile phone towers does indeed increase health risks, including the prevalence of cancer. Older studies say there is no risk. More recent studies, like the NTP rat study, show there is a significant risk.

One of the most telling and perhaps most disturbing indicators of the dangers of cell phone towers are the cancer clusters and groupings of other diseases that frequently spring up around them.

One of the key reasons that evidence is limited is because cell phone technology is quite new. It's only been widely available for the last few decades, which means that we, as yet, can't know the long-term health impacts associated with them. Additionally because there are so many cell phone towers with more and more springing up every year, we're all exposed to the EMR they emit. There's just no getting away from them.

Because of this, as research continues, it's impossible to get a genuine control group of people who are not exposed to EMF's and therefore who are not in some ways affected. Having said that, independent studies were carried out and are telling. Studies have been undertaken across the globe, with many occurring throughout Europe.

A French study from 2003, for example, reported that people living within 300 meters of mobile phone antennas base stations reported high levels of fatigue, sleep disturbance, general feelings of discomfort, headaches, consideration problems, anxiety and depression, memory loss, visual disturbances, auditory disturbances, mood swings, cardiovascular disorders, dizziness and loss of balance.

They found similar results in Spain, Germany, and the UK. Aside from the increased incidences of these common symptoms, many of these studies also uncovered a disturbing correlation between proximity to a mobile phone base station and incidences of cancer. And these aren't just a few cases of childhood cancer or even brain tumors, which would be horrific enough, but the cancer clusters and other clusters of serious illnesses and diseases, uncovered by these studies, afflict people of every age, ethnicity, and social status. We know from these studies that nobody is safe from the health risks of living near a mobile phone base station.

One German study, for example, found that the number of newly developing cancer cases was significantly higher among people who lived during the past 10 years within 400 meters of a base station. The same study highlighted other disturbing facts. Firstly, the study group fell ill on average eight years earlier than the control group outside the 400 meter zone. Secondly, this particular study showed that within just five years of the base station beginning to transmit, the risk of getting cancer, if you lived within 400 meters of the station, tripled, compared to the risk of those people living outside the 400 meter radius.

A study in the UK looked at seven clusters of cancer and other serious illnesses reportedly occurring around cell phone masts. Investigation into the seven sites showed significantly higher incidences of some different cancers, brain hemorrhages, high blood pressure, among other illnesses, within 400 yards of the mobile phone base stations. The Warwickshire site showed a large cluster of 31 cancers in a single street! The results for that same Warwickshire site also revealed that approximately a quarter of 30 members of staff employed at a special school within sight of the 90-foot mobile phone mast are known to have cancerous tumors since 2000. Another quarter had chronic health problems during the same period.

Many studies have been conducted to the dangers of mobile phone towers, and the evidence is quite clear. So, although there are an awful lot of people, including healthcare professionals, scientists, government officials, and business managers, who will tell you that those studies are hokum and that there is no danger from living close to a mobile phone tower, nor from using your smart phone all the time, the evidence is there for you to see.

What is interesting is that across the world, as people become more aware of the dangers surrounding them, the value of property near mobile phone base stations (and high voltage electricity towers) continues to drop, and that has to be a good thing. It means people are waking up to the dangerous reality in which we live, and they are making a choice.

But the money people are getting smarter. It's no longer enough to look out for nearby cell towers and stay away. Why? Because they've started to disguise and hide them. I've seen them in France. Quite the latest in Techno Deco. Look out for cell towers in the form of pine trees or palms sprinkled along freeways and busy intersections. They disguise them as rocks, trees, buildings, chimneys, and hide them in church towers.

When you think about the strategic location of most village churches in the center of town, this presents a scary concept. Even so, strategically placed cell towers are everywhere, even in abandoned, medieval villages in deepest France. All over the world in fact. Look up cancer clusters and you'll know what I speak of.

Why any religious place would condone this practice makes one wonder? Or not. My point being, you can't even see most of these cell towers. So, to check your safety level you need to get an EMF detector, which is definitely one of the best investments I've made. I've been in the country, in places that look pristine, like next to a river in the middle of nowhere, where nobody would blame you for thinking you're in Hobbit country. Yet, when I measured my surroundings I got a big surprise. What looks like paradise is often hell in disguise. You might be thinking there's no cell tower anywhere near you, while you're sizzling like an overcooked steak. Basically, though, if you can see the mast it's too close to you. And even if you can't, unless it is more than 5 km away, you're exposed. Phone masts impact people big time.

CONFLICTING INFORMATION

Conflicting information - and the careful and absolute control over what information reaches the general population all contributes to keeping us in the dark. If we stay ignorant, we'll just keep on buying and using all these lethal devices. The fat cats will keep getting fatter, and we'll continue to suffer. And our children will suffer. And, assuming that they by some miracle don't suffer from the infertility associated with EMF exposure, our children will produce children who will suffer even more.

Doctor Joel Maskowitz of the University of California, Berkeley's Center for Family and Community Health, said, "I think we're undergoing a major global health experiment unprecedented, perhaps, in the history of the planet." He goes on to say that similar to exposing the effects of smoking or the awful results of asbestos inhalation, it could take up to 20 years to convince consumers, who have essentially been conditioned to have faith in their devices, about what he believes are the adverse health effects of wireless radiation.

How is this for conflicting information? Radio frequency energy, or non-ionizing radiation, has been proven, beyond doubt, to increase the risk of cancer, and, in x-ray form, for example, is known to pose a threat to unborn babies, in that the radiation can interrupt, mutate, or otherwise change their cell growth. The National Cancer Institute, however, claims, "there is currently no evidence that non-ionizing radiation increases cancer risk."

PROVING THE LIE

"There is every indication that cell phones cause brain tumors, salivary gland tumors and eye cancer. Yet, because the cell phone industry provides a substantial proportion of research funding, this reality is hidden from the general public. The Interphone Study, a 13-country research project, substantially funded by the cell phone industry has consistently shown that use of a cell phone protects the user from risk of a brain tumor! Does anything more need to be said? It is time that fully independent studies be funded by those governmental agencies whose charter is to protect its citizens so that the truth about the very damaging health hazards of microwave radiation becomes clear and well known." - L. Lloyd Morgan, BS Electronic Engineering. Director Central Brain Tumor Registry of the United States, Member Bioelectromagnetics Society, Member Brain Tumor Epidemiological Consortium *

Governments, health professionals, and scientists with a vested interest in the outcome of studies deny the existence of Electromagnetic Hypersensitivity Syndrome and the dangers of Electromagnetic Radiation. Yet, they make and enforce safety policies against it. Why would you waste money and resources making policies and conducting research into something you claim doesn't exist or has no harmful effects? Many governments who deny any claims to the truth that exposure to excessive levels of EMR have whole policy documents surrounding public and workplace safety with regards to electromagnetic radiation, and radio frequencies.

ANECDOTAL EVIDENCE

There's an insane amount of anecdotal evidence, some of which is collected and collated by scientific bodies. Other evidence of the anecdotal variety is everywhere, with many people starting their own website blogs to detail their own experience, even without a formal diagnosis. It's not just the general public either.

More health professionals, businessmen, and public figures are standing up and telling the world about their experience with EHS. As mentioned you've got Gro Harlem Brundtland, former director-general of the WHO. Matti Niemelä, who was Nokia's chief technology officer. A former Ericsson cell phone engineer, Per Segerback. And countless others. People are starting to speak out about their symptoms, from TV producers and sound engineers to health professionals, businesswomen, IT professionals, scientists, medical students, priests, surgeons, personal trainers, DJs - the list is endless – and it's not just 'hippy nutjobs', hypochondriacs, or people with poor general health who are making stuff up or blaming their non-specific symptoms on EHS because they don't know what else to do. From the anecdotal evidence we can see that EHS can hit anyone.

While many detractors claim that symptoms are too vague and non-specific, because there are many of them and they can mimic other conditions, what's interesting is that all across the world these people and their anecdotal evidence all share the same symptoms. They all report experiencing the same kind of ill health and they also experienced some relief from their symptoms when they reduce the amount of electromagnetic radiation they expose themselves to.

THE INCREASED RISK TO CHILDREN

The Venice Resolution, initiated by the International Commission for Electromagnetic Safety (ICEMS) on June 6, 2008, and now signed by nearly 50 peer reviewed scientists worldwide, states in part...

"We are compelled to confirm the existence of non-thermal effects of electromagnetic fields on living matter, which seem to occur at every level of investigation from molecular to epidemiological. Recent epidemiological evidence is stronger than before. We recognize the growing public health problem known as electro-hypersensitivity. We strongly advise limited use of cell phones, and other similar devices, by young children and teenagers, and we call upon governments to apply the Precautionary Principle as an interim measure while more biologically relevant exposure standards are developed." - Prof. Livio Giuliani, PhD. Spokesperson, International Commission for Electromagnetic Safety (www.icems.eu). Deputy Director, Italian National Institute for Worker Protection and Safety, East Venice and South Tyrol; Professor, School of Biochemistry of Camerino University, Italy.

Babies, and children are at a far greater risk from the affects of EMF exposure than adults. Aside from the results from many studies, this does make sense. Pre-adult, your body is still growing. Your biological systems still developing and maturing. So children are less resilient. Less able to withstand the stresses of EMF exposure at the cellular level. Hence, it doesn't take much exposure for developing bodies to become saturated.
And, because the Digital Age is still in its infancy, we don't know all the long-term effects yet. Our children are exposed to higher levels of radiation than any previous generation. Exposure starts in the womb, and continues for their entire lives. And nobody actually knows how much damage that's going to do.

What we do know is bad enough. This cumulative exposure can irradiate a child's bone marrow. And cause untold damage for their entire lives. Including fertility problems, major behavioral problems, DNA damage, EHS, and other debilitating conditions. This is what we're doing to our children every time we let them use our laptops or tablets. Every time we buy them a mobile phone. Every time we let them play on a games console. Every time we let them watch a movie sitting too close to the TV. And just think of the potential damage to unborn babies. Those tiny, fragile bundles of growing cells exposed to the same EMF levels as their mothers. This is why some countries, like France, decided to remove Wi-Fi in their schools. And even some universities, like Lakehead University in Canada are Wi-Fi-free.

It's also why we need more countries to follow suit. And why parents should be more aware of the dangers and take appropriate precautions. For example, most major kid's brands push wireless baby monitors on new parents. Unfortunately, they produce large amounts of EMF pollution. And you place these beside your infant's crib, surrounding your tiny baby in an arc of radiation. Not good. So downgrade your tech around your kids. Hard-wire everything. And, if you don't need it, get rid of it. Our parents and grandparents didn't need these fancy modern conveniences to raise healthy children. Do you?

"...Children are more severely affected because their brains are developing and their skulls are thinner. A two-minute call can alter brain function in a child for an hour, which is why other countries ban their sale or discourage their use under the age of 18. In contrast, this is the segment of the population now being targeted here in a $2 billion U.S. advertising campaign that views 'tweens' (children between 8 and 12 years old) as the next big cell phone market. Firefly and Barbie cell phones are also being promoted for 6 to 8-year-olds...." - Paul J. Rosch, MD - Clinical Professor of Medicine and Psychiatry, New York Medical College; Honorary Vice President International Stress Management Association; Diplomate, National Board of Medical Examiners; Full Member, Russian Academy of Medical Sciences; Fellow, The Royal Society of Medicine; Emeritus Member, The Bioelectromagnetics Society

THE RISK TO ANIMALS

Think only humans are at risk from EHS? You are wrong. As I've already said, it's every living thing. Every single living cell on the planet – and that includes animals and plants. We already know that unnatural EMFs are harmful to human health.

We knew it back in the 1930's, so even if we didn't have science to back it up, it makes sense that electromagnetic radiation causes damage to other living creatures, too. One of the biggest problems is that there are few recent truly independent scientific studies. There are plenty that were commissioned by government agencies, and carried out in the late 70s and 80s. There are also plenty of recent studies and data. Again, none collected in a way that adheres to recognized scientific evidence. And, as already mentioned, there's a huge collection of anecdotal and observational data, but again, without strict adherence to the prescribed scientific method, much of the scientific community dismiss the results or proclaim that the data gathered has shown the need for more studies.

Here's a little of what we do know. Now, animals, including your beloved pets, suffer many of the same symptoms we do. Isn't it awful to think that using your tablet, playing on a wireless game pad, or browsing Netflix on your smart TV is causing at least some of those dreadful symptoms in your dog or cat? Even your poor rabbit or hamster. All animals are at risk. I mean, we're all animals, so if EMR is bad for us, it's bad for other creatures, too.

Aside from the obvious (or sometimes not so obvious) outward physical or behavioral symptoms, some species are affected in other ways. Creatures that rely on the Earth's natural electromagnetic field for navigation, for example, are exceptionally sensitive to EMR from any source. This includes a lot of marine and fresh water wildlife, including salmon, turtles, and other species that migrate or travel across a large range or territory.

It's not just those confined to land and water, either. Many species of birds navigate by the feel of the Earth's natural electromagnetism. And even species that don't navigate by it are exceptionally sensitive to it. The same goes for a lot of insects – most notably, bees.

There have been many studies on the effects of EMFs on bees. Generally, results show that bees have a serious adverse reaction to their presence. Starling W. Childs, M. S., geologist and forestry consultant and adjunct faculty member at the Yale School of Forestry and Environmental Studies tells us that bees, like so many other species, operate in the naturally occurring magnetic field generated by the Earth. He goes on to explain that bees use this background magnetism to find food, to communicate, and to engage in their colonies.

When you introduce artificial fields, like those generated by cell phones, Wi-Fi, and pretty much any other piece of active electronic equipment, you have an immediate and serious impact on bee colonies. The presence of EMFs distorts the bees' perception, their ability to follow lay lines and scent paths, and their ability to use the sun as an additional navigational source. So, they get confused, can't communicate with the rest of the colony, and often cannot find their way back to the colony.

Studies have documented this and many authorities around the globe are certain that EMR (Electromagnetic Radiation) is the cause of CCD, or Colony Collapse Disorder. For example, a study conducted in Spain took multiple honeybee colonies and used half as a control group, unexposed to EMF's. The other half had a cordless phone base in the vicinity of their colonies, which emits a level of EMF's considered 'safe'. Once established, the worker bees were taken 800 meters from their colonies and released. The control groups made it back to their colonies within 30 minutes. The bees exposed to the excessive EMF, however, had a whole world of problems. Some sluggishly found their way back in an hour, but between 30 and 40 percent of every exposed colony failed to make it back at all.

Other studies have shown that the navigational and societal impact is so great that after just 10 days of exposure, worker bees leave their colonies altogether. In these studies, after 10 days of steady exposure, only the queen, her eggs, and a few immature worker bees were left in the hive. All of these observational studies clearly show that the ever-increasing presence of EMR is causing honeybee colonies to collapse and their numbers to decline.

And it doesn't stop there. In colonies that don't suffer from CCD but do suffer from EMF exposure, queen bees are documented as producing an average of just 100 eggs a day, compared to the usual 350 eggs per day. Additionally, the bees take longer to reach maturity, are smaller when they do reach maturity, and are slower, less efficient, and less productive. The honeycomb is also smaller and weighs less.

The potential impacts are devastating if we don't take action. Yes, we could live without honey, so it's not that big of a deal, right? Wrong. Bees are pollinators. If we lose the pollinators, we won't be able to keep the planet fed long-term. You simply can't pollinate enough plants by hand to keep the world's population in fruit and vegetables. So just think about that for a minute. The Digital Age that we all revel and indulge in is actually killing off our food sources. What do we do then? And if it's happening to bees, it's happening to other crucial insect species, too.

Migratory birds. They use the natural magnetic field of the Earth, following lay lines or the Earth's geomagnetism. EMFs throw them off, completely messing with their senses. Sometimes, it can delay migration, meaning the birds struggle to make the long journeys in tougher conditions, as the weather changes, and many more juveniles may not manage the more challenging migration. And even if they do, the EMFs can throw the flock completely off course. It's increasingly common for EMR to be so disruptive to a flock's flight pattern, that it draws the birds right into the power lines and telecommunications towers. The birds either fly into the masts themselves or the lines. This is known as a bird strike and results in huge numbers of birds dying each year.

Bats. While most people don't like them, they are important little creatures and help to naturally control insects that we consider pests and disease carriers, like mosquitoes. Did you know a bat consumes 80% of its own bodyweight in insects every single night? Unfortunately, they detect their prey using sonar. Essentially, like bees, they operate on the Earth's natural background magnetism, and use it to find their food and to communicate. The huge influx of EMF over the last few decades has resulted in a rapid decline in numbers, with some species being close to extinction.

Goodness, there are so many species seriously affected, they'd fill several volumes all on their own. So we'll leave the animal world alone for now, and take a look at what's happening to our environment.

THE RISK TO THE ENVIRONMENT

"There are many examples of the failure to use the precautionary principle in the past, which have resulted in serious and often irreversible damage to health and environments. Appropriate, precautionary and proportionate actions taken now to avoid plausible and potentially serious threats to health from EMF are likely to be seen as prudent and wise from future perspectives." - Professor Jacqueline

McGlade - Executive Director, European Environmental Agency Advisor to European Union countries under the European Commission

It's not just the fauna – it's the flora, too. In fact, EMF's affect the entire planet. Studies show that vegetation, including fruit and vegetable plants, grow slower, are smaller at maturity and frequently show signs of deformity, along with having a substantially higher concentration of free radicals. These exposed plants also contain a much higher concentration of alanine, which is a substance that indicates stress in plants. A significant reduction in seed production, reduced germination rates, and lower crop yields have all been thoroughly documented in relation to EMF exposure, including low-level radiation like that emitted from power lines.

There's also the well-documented corona that occurs in vegetation close to power lines. It's most common with plants and trees with spiky or segmented leaves. These types of plants that are subjected to EMF exposure develop corona, where the leaves turn dry and crispy. Often, the leaves change color, turning yellow, brown, or grey, and they curl up and die, which hinders the growth and productivity of the plant as a whole. So, not only are we killing off our pollinators, we're also decreasing our crop yield. Again, we're destroying our food sources (not to mention our health and our planet) for a bit more time on Facebook, or an app and a smart thermostat that lets you turn the kettle on while you're still in the office. Is it worth it?

PART 2 – HOW TO DIAGNOSE AND TREAT ELECTRO-SENSITIVITY

"It is not the strongest of the species that survives, nor the most intelligent that survives. It is the one that is most adaptable to change." - Charles Darwin

MY JOURNEY

The short version of a very long story goes like this: At the edge of forty, my ex partner and I ended our 9-year relationship. I sold my house and all my belongings and found myself without identity, without certainty. Then, in 2009, during 6 months of deliberate 'time-wasting' in Sydney's Bondi Beach, I met Fabrice and moved from Australia to France. In an attempt to do something with my life, I started writing. I became a location-independent writer living a sort of idyllic, bohemian existence and I was happy. And for a while there, things were looking pretty rosy.

In 2012 I caught a flu that came with swollen glands and a massive bronchial infection that wouldn't go away. Around 6 months later, strange things started to happen to my body. I began to notice some weird sensations when I spoke on the phone, especially heat on the side of my head and tingling on my face whenever I spent too much time on the computer. I thought little of it back then and carried on using my gadgets, until I developed a rather long list of mystery symptoms and circumstances I couldn't make sense of. Here's a brief summary:

Months of unexplained vague illness and finally, four weeks in bed without being able to move, get up, talk, walk or think.

A few minutes of working on the computer using Wi-Fi, had my face burning. Not a problem, I thought... I'll buy a Himalaya Salt Lamp at the health shop to diffuse negative ions in the room...that'll do the trick. Wrong!

Electro Static – noticed I'd been getting more of a regular zapping over the years. Car doors, clothes hangers, anything polyester in clothing have become off limits for including metal door handles etc. Always have to double check so as not to receive a massive jolt. And believe me, they got bigger!!! Kissing when one is electro static? Impossible!!!

Multitudes of ambulance trips (because I couldn't keep my head up, or walk or do anything), yet blood tests always came back clean.

Saw multitudes of doctors who didn't listen and didn't have a clue.

A 2-week collapse (with mystery seizures) when a friend visited from Australia. I was incapable of entertaining, going out and participating in anything as I couldn't manage it. She didn't understand. How could she?

A total energy collapse at my mum's place after being on a plane for only 2 hours. Took 2 weeks of bed to recover.

I would sleep around 12-14 hours per day, and wake up exhausted, vague, foggy. Chronic Fatigue anyone???

Various digestion problems, sudden food intolerances, leaky gut.

Difficulty speaking, struggling to construct a sentence.

Hearing: When people spoke to me they sounded as though they were speaking in slow motion. Weird!!!

Memory loss

Vertigo

Extremely dry, crocodile skin

Rapid deterioration of vision

Muscle spasms and twitches (all day long), not the kinds you get when lacking in magnesium for example. These feel like random, electrical flicks all over the body.

Heart problems: palpitations, tachycardia or tachyarrhythmia episodes

Skin sensitivity (tingling, burning or itching) on the face and scalp or arms and/or the forearm, or the hand holding the mobile phone or the computer mouse.

Headaches associated typically with stiffness and pain in the neck.

Intolerance to noise, in particular to background noise.

Visual disturbances like blurred vision

Dizziness when standing

Pulsating, throbbing sensation near the brain stem when standing from a seated position.

Unable to balance when walking

Muscle disorders (myalgia, spasms, twitching) and/or joints (arthralgia, stiffness)

Muscle weakness (at one stage I couldn't even lift my arms)

Loss of muscle tone

Cognitive impairment, like attention deficit and concentration and loss of short-term memory

Vegetative symptoms

Tightness in the chest

Urinary problems (frequent urination, felt like a full time job)

Depressive tendencies

Crying at the drop of a hat

Tight Psoas muscle

Hypoglycemia (low blood sugar)

Adrenal Burnout

Sudden drops in blood pressure

Shaking and body tremors

Behavioral disorders like irritability and verbal abuse

Intolerance to high histamine foods like tomatoes, avocados, bananas (foods I always loved without a problem in the past).

The list goes on...

Throughout the next year or so I felt increasingly frail and could no longer do normal things like go for a daily walk in the streets of Marseille. A simple trip to the supermarket, a few hundred meters from our home, would wipe me out for hours. A glass or two of wine would cause a massive hangover for days!!! I became increasingly intolerant to certain foods. Sometimes my energy was so low I couldn't get out of bed, or even lift my head off the pillow to the point where my husband had to walk me to the bathroom. By this stage I was mostly housebound and bedridden without knowing why and forced to 'disconnect' in more ways than one as my health continued on a downward spiral.

I continued to shuffle from doctor to doctor without any clear diagnosis. Countless ambulance trips to the emergency room continued, countless blood tests were a waste of time and money as all the doctors came back with the same response 'There's nothing wrong with you'.

One day, my Osteopath gave me the name of an alternative doctor in Marseille. After a rather long consultation, he suggested I might be sensitive to Electromagnetic Frequencies. The idea was entirely new to me, and his comment seemed a little far-fetched, but I did some research and found an article about an environmental illness specialist in France who knows how to diagnose people with EHS. Three months later, I was in Dr Belpomme's clinic in Paris. It was 2014. And at the time, I was one of 12 000 people in France officially diagnosed with Electromagnetic Hypersensitivity Syndrome (EHS). *Et Voila!* Now I had my diagnosis. But what about a cure?

For lack of assistance and options I began to self-navigate. I read, studied and applied various natural healing methods that helped me to adapt to the modern world. A world that, as yet, wasn't ready to hear about my situation. And although, having no where to go for help and nobody to talk to for lack of understanding (those were dark times), I soon came to know that in every adversity, there is a major benefit. Any chronic illness is debilitating and painful in more ways than one. The benefit is usually a huge dose of personal growth. So years of waiting for a diagnosis followed by frantically hunting for answers as to why this 'plane crash happened in my backyard', lead me in a new direction. Every aspect of my previous life changed, and things would never be the same again.
I digress. Back to my journey.

Regardless of the fact that EHS is physiological not psychological in origin, I didn't want to tell people about my condition. I didn't want to tell my friends that I was no longer the carefree, globetrotting freedom seeker I used to be. That instead I'd become a modern-world refugee. Someone who can no longer fly on an airplane (a flight can wipe me out for weeks). Someone who can no longer take the train. For whom driving is a challenge. And going to a supermarket presents a nightmare. Coffee with friends? Forget it.

My life in France with the love of my life was now a beautiful parenthesis, rather than the whole truth. Actually I did tell some people, a small handful of friends. Sad to say they reacted badly out of ignorance, or worse, they didn't believe me, avoided the topic entirely and never again asked me about my health condition over the next few years. Ouch!

Being EHS has had a dramatic impact on my life. I had to give up my online work. We had to sell our home in Marseille. And I've dropped out of most of my online social networks. When I do go online to touch base with friends I keep it brief. No time to connect on a deeper level with friends living on the other side of the planet. Plus I rarely go out to socialize, and when I do it's only for short periods of time.

EMOTIONAL AND SOCIAL IMPACT OF EHS

When I tell people I have EHS, most have no idea what I'm talking about. Or what it feels like on any emotional and physical level. So I'll try to draw you a picture. Actually these days things are looking a little brighter... but to give you an idea, this is how things used to look...

EHS feels like a sense of abandonment by the world one was born to.

It feels as though I'm living life in a bubble. Always thinking of protection against the environment. Avoidance behavior on every level. The environment against me.

Most people don't realize that many people with EHS are disabled. Some have lost everything, including their jobs, homes and their savings. Some have even lost their spouses and families for lack of understanding.

For example, I no longer have a regular income. Neither does my husband, as he is too busy looking after me. There is no health-care or social security payment that covers me because as yet, EHS is not recognized by the French government.

So far, I have managed to find ways to live with EHS without working a full-time job, in order to function around it. Currently we're living off the sale of our apartment in Marseille, the sales of my books and my superannuation savings in Australia. The only way I could touch those, was by getting two EHS aware French doctors to sign a form stating that I am, in fact, disabled.

At one stage I was homeless, with no permanent base for 4 years moving between Marseille, Grasse, and Bosnia (my mum's place) and back to France looking for an unpolluted or less polluted *zone blanche* or 'white zone' to take refuge. For a while, I even lived and slept in our shielded old camping car.

Right now we're in France as things are still bearable in our region. But how long before it becomes unbearable and there's nowhere left to hide? By 2020 5G will be 'rolled out' all over Europe. Many times, I've wondered about what I'll do to make a living? How will I survive? Where will we live? How will all of this impact my relationship with my husband? And how will EHS impact me when I'm older and less able to look after myself?

Today, a number of EHS people live in remote places like caves, forests, and desert islands. In a documentary on EHS people in France, they interviewed an ex-Air France airhostess who was in her late 60's. After a life-long career of flying around the world she got sick and is now forced to live in a cave (thick stone blocks EMF's), because it's the only place she can sleep and escape her torturous headaches.

Another woman quit her home to live in a caravan in the forest. Her husband sees her once a week when he brings food and supplies. He can't join her as he has to work, so she lives alone (broke my heart that one).

Another woman sleeps in her shielded car every night... the only way she can get sleep away from the neighbors Wi-Fi.

Unfortunately most people don't have the 'luxury' of being able to drop off the face of the earth and live in a rural community. Most people have jobs and kids at school, families and friends. All these things are normal and equate to having a normal life, so they can't or won't just up and leave and become a hermit. They have no other options. They are stuck, with mortgages and bills to pay. And this only increases anxiety, panic and frustration when it comes to EHS. If I had children to support I don't know what I would do.

Just being around people is exhausting; often the simple act of talking or trying to explain my situation to people feels like too much, which is why this ex-social butterfly is now a semi-hermit. There's no question of a social life when people's 'smart' phones are the new crack cocaine. I miss hanging out with people and friends, without the relentless phone fondling. I miss real conversations, catching up for coffee or a drink.

Which is why I'm housebound most of the time. Always having to decline invitations to go out for fear of seeming like a no fun pain in the ass. One time, my cousin organized an impromptu BBQ. Within 5 minutes they had switched on their Bluetooth speaker for music, which under normal circumstances would seem fun and normal right? Wrong. Bluetooth makes me feel as though my face is on fire. I politely asked them to switch it off. They did, which meant no music for anybody. How does one win friends and influence people when they have EHS?

I used to love going for long walks but I haven't walked for years. Anything more than 10 minutes feels like climbing Mount Everest. And just 'thinking' of having to walk anywhere puts my nervous system into a fight or flight state. The less I move the more my muscles waste away. Flesh hanging from bones. No muscle tone. Not to mention episodes of drastic weight loss, which makes me look scary to say the least.

With this, comes the inevitable depression. I use the word 'depression' in a loose sense, as I've never been depressed in my life. And when doctors ask if I'm depressed I laugh because NO, I'm not depressed. And YES I do go through some super-dark, hairy, shitty, bottom of the barrel health moments, as anyone with a chronic illness can tell you is normal. Do I want or need anti-depressants? Absolutely not! What else...

I avoid big surface shopping malls and supermarkets like the plague. All those neon lights, cash registers, cues, and people fixated on the phones.

Emotionally EHS can feel incredibly isolating. One can feel pretty much alone and very different to the rest of the population. I feel my life, as it was… was stolen from me. There's a sense of being misunderstood by pretty much everyone. That, as a person in love with her freedom, it was taken from me. I have become a prisoner, an EMF Refugee. Someone who can no longer do normal things others take for granted. Any chores I need to do I do in small bursts so as not to deplete my daily energy budget… for if I overdo things, I collapse in a heap and my brain turns to slush.

Most days I can't do anything but be in a vegetative state - radiation poisoning seems to have infiltrated my body but also my mind, my spirit, my soul, and my entire life. Life feels like a constant challenge for survival. Yes, definitely no thriving going on.

I can't travel or take public transport without major health challenges.

Driving is an obstacle as motors produce electricity.

So is cooking on an electric stove for more than a few minutes.

No electric gadgets of any kind are possible. Including hairdryers, electric toothbrushes etc.

Protective, ugly clothing for shielding purposes is a must throughout the day (I don't wear the stuff when on occasion I do get out, although I probably should). Irony: I've always loved hats – once they were my trademark accessory item, and now I HAVE to wear a protective hat lined with Swiss shield fabric most days. Protective gloves are a must when typing on the keyboard.

I use curtains to shield rooms, bedding too, which can't be washed too often (yuckypoo!), because the more you wash it, the less it works as it affects the silver and copper fibers throughout the fabric. Needless to say, at 50 euros per meter, these items are a pain in the ass and extremely costly.

Then there's the getting somewhere and back through a maze of cell towers, people, cars all connected to 'the source'.

A casual outing in the city is loaded with problems. Most places have free Wi-Fi (extra fast/powerful) now. Visiting friends is the same. If they do visit me, (which happens rarely when you live in a shielded camping car and have no fixed address) it can frazzle me for days. I have to remind them to turn off their phones. They still don't get it. Who can be bothered explaining one's health when nobody 'gets it'... or worse, they pretend to be empathic, nodding away, while checking their smartphone for messages. These days I'm learning to forgive those who struggle with understanding.

In fact, I've only experienced two occasions of people turning off their phones when visiting. Both times, it was unexpected as they were more acquaintances than friends. Albeit very thoughtful and kind ones.

Like I said, some friends don't believe I'm sick. Others have dropped away. My relentless posts about 5G on Facebook aren't helping. People prefer photos of a coffee and croissant in a French café. Know what I mean?

So you see, EHS affects every part of life, body and soul on every level. And it feels brutal. I used to get pissed off. A lot. Especially as nobody ever asked me if they could put cell towers on practically every inch of the planet. Did they ask you? Didn't think so. Even if they did, what would you/we have said?

So now I'm bubble girl who lives life in a bubble and stays indoors for months on end. One 'friend', in particular, keeps asking me (via facebook) about the 'fun' things I'm planning to do this weekend, this year/summer/Christmas/New Year etc. Sometimes I wonder if she does it on purpose. More than likely, she is ignorant and has no clue. Some people are incapable of empathy, and that's just how it is.

Occasionally though, the dark veil lifts during moments when I'm doing something normal, when I force myself to go out - when I want to forget and be like everybody else... until some physical symptom brings me back to earth and I'm reminded that spontaneity is a thing of the past.

KEY SYMPTOMS TO LOOK FOR

You might think you're ok. You don't have any significant symptoms, and that long days stuck at the computer just give you a bit of a headache, like everyone else. However, it could be something more. You know when you've been working online for a few hours and you start to feel nauseous? Or when you don't take regular breaks from your computer and your face and extremities start to tingle. Or you inexplicably get excessively hot while you're playing on your iPad/talking on your smartphone or cordless phone. Well, those are all common markers for EHS. When you experience any of those symptoms, your body, including your brain is being negatively affected by your exposure to electromagnetic radiation.

Do many of the symptoms of EHS appear to be vague and non-specific? Yes they do. Could they realistically be the result of other conditions or just an unhealthy lifestyle? Yes they could. So once you've eliminated other conditions, and you know your lifestyle isn't particularly unhealthy, what's next? Could the symptoms you're experiencing simply be all in your head? Yes, they could. Could it be that you're simply letting your fear of modern life create imagined symptoms? It's possible. Could your symptoms simply be a physical manifestation of your anxiety? Yes, they could. But don't assume these things. And once you've eliminated poor mental health, what are you left with? EHS.

So why are the symptoms so widespread? Why do they vary so much? The answer is very simple. Electromagnetic radiation negatively impacts every system in the body. That's right. It impacts the nervous, immune, and endocrine system, among others. It completely throws your body out of homeostasis, and when so much of the body's essential systems are malfunctioning, or at least not functioning optimally, you'll present with an array of what appears to be non-specific symptoms.

One of the key symptoms you'll experience with EHS are headaches. They can be mild, or they can be intolerable migraines that last for days. Commonly, you will often get 'tension headaches' with pain running along the sides of the head and at your temples.
Palpitations are another symptom. Heart palpitations give you a frightening, unpleasant feeling in your chest. Your heart pounds or feels like it's giving an extra beat, or wants to jump right out of your chest.

With exposure to EMF, you'll likely experience burning sensations or actual burns, particularly of the skin on the face and hands, and you may see redness, get unexplained rashes, and tingling sensations.

Sleep will be an issue. You may suffer from extreme tiredness - feeling like you're simply too exhausted to stand up or do much of anything - but you'll find it hard to sleep. You'll experience long bouts of insomnia. Or you'll be able to fall asleep, but you'll wake up regularly throughout the night, your sleep will be light and dreamless, and you'll wake up feeling just as tired as you did when you went to bed.

You may well hear ringing or humming that nobody else can hear. While this may be tinnitus, it could also be the mystery 'hum' that only EMF-sensitive individuals can supposedly hear.

Your brain. You'll undoubtedly feel like you're experiencing an alarming cognitive decline. Your brain will feel "foggy", like you can't think clearly, perhaps like you're experiencing a kind of sedative effect where your brain simply won't function as it did. You'll have trouble remembering - most specifically short-term memory will be a problem. You'll struggle to remember what happened yesterday - or maybe even a few hours ago. And you won' absorb information easily. You'll struggle to concentrate for more than short periods. The most frightening part is that Dr Belpomme warned me of a strong possibility of early onset Alzheimer's.

But know that once you shield yourself, limit your exposure, or get away from EMF altogether, your symptoms will quickly improve - and who knows...with continued avoidance, they may disappear altogether as some people have claimed.

If you suspect you have EHS and don't have the means to get tested, do this: Take yourself out of your immediate environment and go to the most pristine, rural place you can find. Stay there. Camp. Sleep in a tent for a few days or a week or two without any gadgets. Turn off your phone and computer. Better still; find a place with no signal (easier said than done). If your body immediately begins to feel better you're most likely EMF intolerant. Don't have to be Einstein to figure it out.

COMMON SECONDARY SYMPTOMS

Anxiety/Panic Attacks - feeling agitated, panic-stricken, or inexplicably anxious about anything and everything.

A compromised immune system - you'll heal slower than normal, you'll find it harder to fight off illness, and you'll be more prone to catching colds, too. Your body and its immune system are already severely strained from EMF damage, so it'll be far more susceptible to bacteria, viruses, parasites, and other forms of infection.

You may find that, at times, you can't speak coherently - your speech will temporarily be slurred, or you say the wrong words.

You'll also likely experience lightheadedness, vertigo, and nausea on a fairly regular basis.

Because the endocrine system, which manages your hormone levels, among other things, is so heavily damaged by EMF exposure, mood swings are exceptionally common. You'll feel weepy, full of rage, happy, lethargic, devastated, depressed, helplessly despairing, and sometimes experiencing multiple emotions in rapid succession.

Involuntary movements may not be terribly noticeable, or they could pose a significant issue for you. If you experience this symptom, you'll find your fingers, arms, hands, legs, and feet twitching or jerking randomly without your conscious control (I used to get restless leg syndrome).

Last, but by no means least on this list of the most common secondary symptoms is a loss of productivity. Because your body is so drained and afflicted by the presence of EMFs, you feel tired, unwell, out of balance, and out of sorts - and, of course, when you get sick, you'll take longer to recover than normal people.

If your symptoms worsen, you may find that you're not able to work at all, because you won't be able to tolerate being surrounded by office electronic devices, wireless Internet, and cellphones. And you are unlikely to be able to work remotely, because that implies you'll be working on a computer, or online - and obviously that's out of the question (unless you turn off Wi-Fi, use Ethernet and shield your computer). This can in turn increase your feelings of worthlessness, and you'll become even less productive and more withdrawn.

Evidently, the symptoms are not pleasant, but they can be managed to an extent, with the right diagnosis, the right support, the right environment, and the right nutrition.

IMPORTANT: *Please note that all of these symptoms may have other causes, which should be ruled out by a medical professional before assuming they are exclusively to do with Electromagnetic Hypersensitivity. The symptoms mentioned here are comprised of both well-documented symptoms from various sources and my own observations and should be treated as anecdotal.*

FINDING THE RIGHT DOCTOR

Symptoms are mostly interchangeable. Cases are difficult to diagnose. Sometimes it takes years if you're lucky enough to land a doctor who isn't in the dark ages, someone who listens, is not arrogant, and won't think you're imagining things, or try to prescribe antidepressants or a psychotherapist.

You'll need to find a doctor who thinks outside the square. And it's not easy. Possible though, as they are now beginning to tune it. After years of mystery illness I managed to find not only one but two. One in Marseille who had the insight to suggest I may be intolerant to EMF's and another in Paris, who was, at the time in 2012, the only physician able to properly diagnose EHS.

Problem with most medical doctors is that they are bound by the system. Mostly they they are in the business of prescribing pharmaceutical drugs, not in the business of healing or even diagnosing properly. For that you usually need to see a specialist.

So, finding the right doctor is crucial. There are fewer things more important in your battle with EHS than getting seen by an informed doctor. The sooner the better, so you don't waste precious time wandering from one to another for years with no answers in sight. Now, it's sadly all too likely that your regular GP won't know what you're talking about - or they'll be dismissive. Do not let your doctor fob you off with a diagnosis of 'it's all in your head'. You know your symptoms are real. How? You feel better when you're in a low EMF zone. It's as simple as that. You have done your research. Yes, lots of doctors hate the invention of the Internet - because patients can inform themselves. And that means we don't have to trust blindly in our doctors any more. We can be proactive in our own health management.

First things first - be prepared. Head to your appointment with all your ducks in a row. As mentioned above - do your research. Get all the facts straight - and have actual proof to give to your GP. Doctors are men and women of science - so they're far more likely to respond positively to scientific evidence than emotional appeals. So, find that scientific data and print it out. Make sure the data is real, reputable, and valid. Take it with you and, if your GP is skeptical ask them to read it.

If you're lacking in confidence, take someone you trust with you - someone who can act as a supportive presence, can bolster your confidence, or help explain your situation. At the end of the day, you know your body better than any doctor can. And you're a lot more invested in your health.

If you find that your doctor isn't remotely helpful and dismisses you as ridiculous, it's time to find another one. Don't stand for that attitude - it's your health and your life that you're dealing with - and it's worth far more than a quick dismissal from an ignorant or worse, uncaring general practitioner. Speak to other doctors or try to find a recommendation from other EHS sufferers to find a doctor who is located near you and willing to listen and perform all the necessary tests.

"People have given their health to their doctor, their money to their banker, their soul to the preacher, their children to the school system, and in doing so, have lost the power to control their lives." Rolling Thunder, Native American Medicine Man

FINALLY AN OFFICIAL DIAGNOSIS!

It's not easy to officially diagnose EHS - it takes a lot of tests and a considerable amount of time. Your doctor will need to take a full medical history, and will need to study your diet and lifestyle. Then, once he/she has a full picture of your life and a full list of your
symptoms and their supposed triggers, your doctor will need to eliminate all the other potential causes of each of your symptoms.

Certain mineral and vitamin deficiencies can mimic some of the symptoms of EHS. You'll also likely undergo scans, blood tests, x-rays, and a battery of other tests to eliminate tumors, problems with your organs, rare bacteria, parasitic infections, thyroid dysfunction, dietary issues, and a whole host of other potential causes.

If your test results show any of these issues, even if they are borderline, they'll require treatment and time to see if your symptoms improve. Once it's confirmed that all the other causes have been eliminated, you may well be asked to undergo controlled exposure-response testing to see if your symptoms can be triggered in a controlled environment. This, however, isn't completely reliable, and many physicians will not rely on this kind of testing alone, and some may not require it at all.

The biggest problem with diagnosing EHS, aside from the challenge of finding a competent, well-informed doctor, is that most doctors know of no conclusive test to confirm the condition at the time of writing. Most doctors cannot simply run a scan, a blood test, or an echocardiogram and get a definitive diagnosis of electromagnetic hypersensitivity. Instead, you and your doctor have to jump through an awful lot of hoops to eliminate all the other possible causes of your symptoms before a diagnosis can be made.

For instance a lack of Magnesium and Spasmophilia show similar symptoms to EHS. Many interrelated symptoms neurological in nature often lead to a misdiagnosis. More often than not, Doctors prescribe antidepressants or anti anxiety drugs, which is probably why the French take more antidepressants than anyone else (apart from Germans, I think). 10 million people in France suffer from Spasmophilia (another mystery illness like CFS and/or Fibromyalgia they have no idea what to do with), hence the Prozac etc. Too easy. Too easily dismissed.

As for me, I finally got a diagnosis via medical imaging and laboratory tests developed by Dr Dominique Belpomme (at the Environmental Medicine Consultation Service of the Alleray-clinical Labrouste in Paris, France), which provided me with definitive proof of the reality of my condition.

HOW EHS IS DIAGNOSED

Here's a brief summary of how it works:

You'll need to have an encephalo scan, a Doppler scan, blood tests and urine tests.

Most patients show a blood hypo perfusion in the cerebral Doppler. This predominant hypo perfusion is in the temporal lobes, particularly in the regions corresponding to the limbic system and/or the thalamus.

Many EHS sufferers show collapsed vitamin D levels in the blood.

About 40% of them show high levels of histamine in the blood.

Still unexplained nearly one in two have high levels of anti-O-myelin antibodies, anti-

Hsp70 and/or anti-Hsp27 in the blood.

Approximately 10% of patients have high levels of S100B protein in the blood, which lead to the opening of the blood-brain barrier.

10% of them have elevated nitrotyrosamine in the blood - which is a marker of oxidative stress - meaning these patients have an overall deficit of antioxidant defenses.

Almost a third of patients show collapsed levels of urinary melatonin.

Inexplicably another third show a significantly increased rate of urinary melatonin.

If you want to read more in-depth information about Dr Belpomme's diagnostic criteria for EHS and Multiple Chemical Sensitivity, here's a link:

https://drive.google.com/file/d/1VnfzSRzmB6loJykb7r-WM8ufOpuo24Wm/view

PART 3 – SELF HELP FOR ELECTRO-SENSITIVE PEOPLE

WHAT ARE THE TREATMENT OPTIONS?

Now let's take a look at ways by which we can help ourselves to heal. First, you need to take care of the basics. There are reams of advice about treating EHS, but it's not all-good advice. I'm not a medical professional, but I know what's worked for me and for a number of other sufferers. There is sadly no definitive cure aside from destroying every cell phone, and cell tower, and bringing down the Internet

– along with destroying every Bluetooth and wireless device - but that's not likely to happen.

It would be cool if we could go back to a simpler time when we communicated via letter, dial-up telephones, and maybe even wired, dial-up Internet (*my choice*). But, as things stand, we're simply going to keep advancing with the insane levels of wireless tech until we reach a crisis point and the truth about the dangers is finally broadcast to everyone. Just like cigarettes.

In fact, it's not too much different from when the ancients used mercury to 'cure' pretty much any disease. It took them a long while to realize just how toxic mercury is. Or the Elizabethans - it took over 100 years for people to realize that the lead-based makeup they were putting on their faces to make themselves fashionably pale was killing them.

One day, the truth will be widely publicized - and the entire world will desperately be turning away from Wi-Fi, cell phones, and all the other harmful emitters of EMF. I'm just hoping, for our sake and for the planet that it won't take too long for the rest of humanity to wake up to the truth.

But, right now, that's not our reality. So, firstly, do everything in your power to limit your exposure. Turn off your cell phone. Turn off your tablet. Only use them when you really need to, if at all. Turn off and unplug every electronic device that you don't actually need. At the very least, go old-school and choose wired tech. Get an Ethernet cable and turn off the wireless mode on your computer - and the wireless capability on your Internet router. Don't forget the seemingly innocuous and convenient wired keyboard and mouse – they are wireless and they are communicating with your computer via radio frequencies. Even cord-less phones...highly dangerous to humans, throw them away - get yourself a cheap, wired version.

Turn your bedroom into a safe zone. Sleep is precious. It's when the body, the cells repair from their daily Wi-Fi onslaught. So the least you can do is remove any electronic device (including your clock radio, TV, computer etc.) from the bedroom. Instead, get a wind-up or battery-powered alarm clock. Don't take your cell phone to bed with you (I'm constantly surprised at the amount of people who sleep with their mobile phone next to their head!!!). Again, if you've got a cordless telephone in there, swap it for a wired, old fashioned one - or get rid of the phone altogether. These are small changes that can help you on your way to managing your condition and/or to avoid getting sick in the first place.

It's not just about eliminating EMF from your environment, however. Managing this potentially debilitating condition is also about helping your body repair itself. You need to actively help your body stay strong, repair the damage that modern life causes, even with limited exposure, and maintain general health. You need to get your body as close to homeostasis as possible - and keep it there. It's about food, natural supplements, detoxing, taking care of your mental health, knowing exactly what you're putting in your body, and getting the right amount and (more importantly), the right type of exercise.

While there are plenty of small changes you can make, depending on the severity of your symptoms, and your current lifestyle, you may need to make some major changes to get the most from your treatment. For instance if you're EMF intolerant, and you live in an urban, polluted environment, think about moving to the country, or perhaps another country. If you can't move because of your career/job, rethink your career/job. It's never too late to re-invent yourself. This may sound over the top and totally unrealistic for most people, I know, but it's your health we're talking about here. Your life is at risk. And nothing else is more important than your life and health. Unfortunately, there is no 'one size fits all' cure for EHS. One can only manage the symptoms by taking truckloads of antioxidants and by protecting oneself.

Best solution: Stay away from EMF pollution. Or limit your exposure. If this is not possible, learn about shielding.

FIRST AID PROTECTION FROM EMF POLLUTION

There is a lot of information on products available. Loads of confusion and misinformation out there. I learned via trial and error. I'm still trying various things. Still buying things that don't work, which is frustrating when you don't have money to throw away. Unfortunately people are cottoning on to this illness and are benefiting via selling products that are dubious to say the least. So be careful. I didn't want to be another person to tell you to buy this or that.

Live in a clean environment: *(easier said than done, I know)*

Mobile phone coverage absence, no Wi-Fi, TNT, digital radio, radar etc.

Choose valleys rather than hilltops, live far from busy roads and railways.

In the city, avoid living on elevated floors with expanding views.

No high voltage power lines within at least 800 meters and no power substation within 50 meters. No Aeolian wind turbines.

Nearest neighbor should be at least 300m from your house.

No chemicals products in your area of habitat (pesticides, detergents, nail adhesives, cleaning products etc.).

In your home:

No Wi-Fi, Bluetooth, DECT (cordless telephone base), home alarm, modem boxes. No microwave, induction cooktops, clock radio, TV, hair dryer, energy-saving bulbs (compact fluorescent bulbs). Use old-fashioned bulbs. Not as eco on your wallet, but omit far less EMF's.

Do not rest or sleep near power cables or plugs as they radiate. Remember that they are integrated into the building (cables in walls). Keep a safe distance from electrical devices: At least 1.50 meters.

Reduce electrical installation pollution:

Grounding and measuring the resistance of earth connections (power points). The measured value should be as low as possible. In any case, less than 10 ohms, if possible, less than 5 ohms, ideally 2 ohms. For your information, the EDF standard (in France) is less than 100 ohms.

Use Shielded cables to prevent electrical fields.

Use Bipolar switches.

Reduce exposure to electromagnetic fields from outside:

Choose windows with high thermal insulation on metal structure.

Inform neighbors about their own electromagnetic pollution. (And about your illness if you think they care :)

If necessary, install shielded cables in walls and floor. There are different possibilities according to the type of pollution and your budget.

For example, we can protect ourselves using different types of armor: special fabrics, paints, wallpaper, carpets, metal mesh gratings on windows and, in emergencies in case of
limited resources, survival blankets.

Measure exposure:

Once the major pollution is neutralized (Wi-Fi, Bluetooth, DECT, Cpl microwave, induction hob, clock radio, TV, computer, hair dryer, energy-saving bulbs), you can opt for a closer diagnosis by using units for measuring EMF's.

The reliability of the results depends on the quality of the meter used. The cost of a professional device can be high, as can bringing in a specialist.

To measure your day-to-day exposure, you can use small units or devices that verify whether or not a particular place is more or less exposed than another. One can find cheaper models from 100 to 300 €. Two devices must be used: one for low frequencies and another for radio frequencies and microwaves.

There's a multitude of devices of varying price range used by people with electro hypersensitivity, which give acceptable readings. However the sensitivity of individuals is often higher than that of the devices, so consider the results with caution.

(I use one that cost 160 €. It's not overpriced, it measures both low and high frequencies and it does the job.)

Before choosing the right shielding:

Shielding should only be considered when all other alternatives have been studied. Moving is often preferable.

For example, there's no point in shielding your home if most of the pollution is coming from the inside, so ensure that the radiation is coming from an outside source. If possible locate it. You can do a Google search to find any local (visible as well as hidden) cell towers.

Be sure to remove anything that would cause radiation inside the room. The "shield" works on the mirror principle (paint, fabrics ...) or by absorption (thick walls ...). So if you shield your home and the inside is polluted (computers, Wi-Fi, electricity etc.), the EMF's will just keep bouncing around the room and doing you more harm in the process. NOT a good idea!!!

Hire a competent electrician to see if your home is properly grounded.

Choosing the right products:

Applying the 'Faraday cage' principle prevents the accidental passing of unwanted waves. We must therefore consider the room or the place to be shielded as a totally sealed box. To do this, the application of a special paint on walls, ceiling and floor is preferable to any other solution. For example, "Y-SHIELD HSF54" costs around 10 € / m2. This paint is black, when applied. If you don't want to live in a black room (who does!!!) then it must be covered with another paint color of choice. Also, it must be earthed. Respect the process indicated in the instructions.

For windows, in addition to windows with thermal insulation, curtains can be made using special shielding fabrics that contain copper and tiny silver threads. The best one by far (as it is biocompatible, is SWISS SHIELD *naturell*, at around € 30 / m2. Mosquito mesh (very fine, made from aluminum) can also do the trick. At night, aluminum shutters are very effective.

For a protected sleep, you can get canopies that look like mosquito nets made with these tissues (to drape over your bed). Note: Under the bed soil treatment is essential if living in an apartment.

Survival blankets offer fairly good shielding performance, but their long-term use is not recommended. They wear out and lose efficiency.

About protective clothing, special attention should be paid. Direct skin contact should be avoided to the extent that metal fibers make up the garment. A protective sheath normally envelops the metal part but this is not always the case. Also, unless your body is completely wrapped in cloth, protection can only be partial. This is not the miracle solution we would like.

Wearing a hat containing silver fabric can sometimes relieve headaches.

The preceding information was created using the experiences of people who are electro hypersensitive. Important note: product trademarks are for identification purposes only. No commercial or any interest exists between manufacturers, dealers of these products and the author of this document.

The information that follows is not advice for treatment. Each person is individual and should seek professional diagnosis and help. Most importantly, they should learn all they can to help themselves.

FOODS TO FORTIFY THE BODY

The question of what to eat and which diet is the healthiest is a perplexing can of worms, and there's no right or wrong answer. One thing is certain. You must regain your health and strengthen your body as much as possible before starting any harsh detox regimes.

A clean diet is probably the most important factor when it comes to health (possibly organic, non GMO, local and seasonal, and rich in antioxidants to combat pollution). Having tried every diet under the sun, I conclude that we are all different, and what works for one person won't work for another. My body works best if I exclude inflammatory foods such as gluten, sugar, wheat and dairy. Some people cut out eggs, but I like them and don't feel they are doing me any harm.

Here's a basic plan I follow:

Vegetables: 8 to 10 servings of vegetables per day. (Eat a variety of colors. e.g. red peppers/tomatoes, green kale, white cauliflower, orange carrots etc.).
Fruit: 1 to 3 servings of local and seasonal fruit.

Whole Grains: Including brown rice (all kinds), quinoa, millet, buckwheat, oatmeal, and amaranth.

Legumes: lentils, chick peas, black beans, split peas, aduki, lima, navy, kidney beans, organic soybeans (nutrients, protein and great fiber for helping in the elimination of wastes and toxins from the body, as well as plentiful nutrients and protein).

Protein: Choose hormone and antibiotic free, organically raised, grass fed animal protein if possible. Fish should be wild. Skip larger fish such as tuna due to the higher mercury content. Instead, choose smaller fish such as sardines, anchovies to provide high quality omega 3 essential fatty acids.

Derive complete protein by combining legumes and whole grains together; you can also add nuts and seeds for good sources of oil and protein. Pumpkin, sesame, sunflower, almonds, pecans, walnuts. As already mentioned, eggs also count.

Oils for cooking and salads: virgin olive oil, coconut oil, and sesame oil.

Herbs: Use garlic, onions, leeks, shallots, curry, oregano, turmeric, parsley and coriander to add flavor and medicinal value to meals.

Drink clean water and herbal tea.

Avoid sugar and additives.

If you must have something sweet, add an occasional teaspoon of honey, pure maple syrup or stevia. I like to eat dry fruit like sundried apricots, dates, figs, prunes.

A basic rule of thumb: If it doesn't heal you, don't eat it.

Also, I cook everything from scratch. Time consuming you might think, but if you organize yourself it's doable. By making a big pot of your favorite soups and stews (keep it simple), you can freeze leftovers and always have a nutritious meal ready to go. Please don't use a microwave (self-explanatory). Your microwave oven should be history by now.

Good hydration with water, free from impurities. Natural spring water is the ultimate, but not practical unless you have your own spring or live near one. I use a carbon filter. It's not ideal but I work with what I can.

Link to a fresh water spring near you ('browse through natural springs around the world'): http://www.findaspring.com/

Some people do well on green juices and smoothies. I guess it depends on your constitution. Because I have a Vata constitution, I prefer warm, cooked, comfort food and follow Ayurveda and/or Chinese Medicine principles. Also if you have any digestive disorders cold, raw and dry foods are more difficult to digest.

Link to an introduction to Ayurvedic vata, pita, kapha doshas: https://www.banyanbotanicals.com/info/ayurvedic-living/learning-ayurveda/vata-pitta-and-kapha/

Link to Healing with Whole Foods book:
https://www.amazon.com/Healing-Whole-Foods-Traditions-Nutrition/dp/1556434308

As I said, we are all unique. I've tried every single diet known to man in an effort to heal. And none of them worked because one size does not fit all. You really need to invest some time into finding out what suits you. Some people do well on a vegan diet, others it makes them sick. Same goes for vegetarian, or paleo, or raw food or whatever. Please experiment. In the end, I encourage you to tap into your body and use your instinct. Nobody knows you as well as you do. For me, the easiest way of knowing what foods my body needs and/or doesn't at any given time is to Energy Test my foods. The same goes for supplements.

Below, Prune Harris demonstrated how to energy self-test what foods can be assimilated and metabolized by your body:
https://www.youtube.com/watch?v=kHEc7LhYOtE

Look into the Dr Terry Wahl's Protocol. This is some of the best info on nutrition I have found, written by a doctor who healed herself from MS by studying exactly what to eat. The protocol is heavy on vegetables and the best way to get 6-9 cups of vegetables in is via green smoothies. I tried it, but my body wasn't ready. Once I heal my gut I will incorporate more green smoothies into my diet, but for now, that's not possible.

Here's a link to her TedX 'Minding your Mitochondria' talk: https://www.youtube.com/watch?v=KLjgBLwH3Wc&vl=en

HELPFUL SUPPLEMENTS

Some thoughts:

If you're in the supplement maze and wondering what on earth to take so you can feel human again, I know how you feel. To be sure, and instead of blindly taking a truck full of supplements you may not need, you should have a test. However, blood tests are not always accurate when it comes to checking your vitamin and mineral levels. Instead, a hair mineral analysis is by far the easiest and most precise way to test for nutritional imbalances.

Some good info here:
https://www.drlwilson.com/articles/HA INTRO.htm

Once you know where you stand you are easier placed to address any imbalances, instead of blindly taking a bunch of supplements without knowing exactly which ones are needed. Don't do what I did and guess. Apart from the fact that it's a waste of time and money, too many synthetic supplements are overwhelming for the system and you won't be doing your liver any favors either. So supplement if you need to. And go for natural food based supplements over synthetic ones. Took me years to realize this one. And thousands of dollars!!! Having said that, most people do well by incorporating the following:

B complex vitamins for nervous system. Be very careful, most vitamins on the market contain deadly synthetic chemicals made from petroleum. They should be avoided. Instead, choose B vitamins made with natural and whole ingredients. (I like natural forms like Spirulina, Bee Pollen and Nutritional yeast)
Omega 3 Fatty Acids (Flaxseed Oil, Fish, Oil)

Magnesium
Zinc
Lion's Mane Mushroom
Moringa
Red Ginseng
Green Tea
Seaweed
Edible green clay (from France)
Chlorella/Spirullina
Calcium
Tumeric
Vitamin D
Digestive Enzymes
Probiotics
Milk Thistle

Most minerals are not digested by the body, so choose ionic minerals. Most calcium tablets on the market for example, contain crushed oyster shells that harden the arteries, or worse, cancer causing ground chalk. Electro-sensitive people need manganese, magnesium, phosphorus and calcium. Also seaweed like Dulce, but rinse the salt as high sodium increases electrical frequencies in the body.

Start reading labels. Don't buy anything that contains artificial colors, flavor enhancers or any other chemical additives like monosodium glutamate, aspartame etc. Better still; don't buy anything that comes in a packet. Opt for fresh food instead!

LIFE-STYLE PRACTICES

As you may or may not know already, healing is a mind/body/spirit undertaking. It's not as easy as changing your diet and taking a bunch of supplements (although it helps), there's a little more to it. Therefore, I invite you to consider implementing some of the following life-style practices. If you are unfamiliar with any of them, do some research and check them out.

You probably won't implement all of them all at once, and some of them may seem a little woo-woo strange right now, but they work, so bear with me and give them a go. You have nothing to lose by going through the list and seeing what feels right for you. Perhaps some of the healing practices will resonate now, and others at a later date. That being said, let's dive right in.

Learn Mindfulness and Meditation techniques
Here's a free online course, no strings attached:
https://palousemindfulness.com/

Yoga. You need to find the method that's right for you, as they all differ. For instance, don't go for an Ashtanga class if it is beyond you (Ashtanga is quite physical). Why not try a Hatha or Restorative, Yin Yoga class instead? With restorative yoga you get to stay in any particular asana (body posture) for as long as needed. Sometimes I stay in the same asana for up to 10-15 minutes, depending on what my body's telling me. It's also why I prefer to practice on my own. Classes are too restrictive in that sense as one is forced to follow someone else's routine and timing. Also, from a practical point of view, when you're unwell, getting to a class is not easy. Occasionally, I've even done it in bed. Try it! It's better than nothing. If you are new to yoga by all means start with a class. If you prefer the group atmosphere, perfect. If you're anything like me, online yoga downloads and/or YouTube work just fine. After a while, you can even create your own routine and change it up whenever you want.

Detox: Look into Hulda Clark's Body Cleanses (parasite, kidney and liver cleanse)

Enemas: As without, so within. A clean colon is vital for healing. Here's some information on coffee enemas (not as scary as it sounds...life-changing, in fact).
https://www.drlwilson.com/articles/COFFEE ENEMA.HTM

Grounding – walk barefoot on soil, grass, the forest, the beach (if not possible, then hardwood or tiled floor)
Book: 'Earthing, the Most Important Health Discovery Ever!'
https://www.amazon.com/Earthing-Most-Important-HealthDiscovery/dp/1591202833

Sleep: Your body restores and repairs itself from EMF damage during sleep. So sleep as much as you can. Most days, I'm in bed before 10pm and up at 7am.

Dry Skin Brushing: Cleans lymphatic system, helps digestion, improves nervous system function, stimulates circulation, strengthens immune system

This should be clear by now, but just in case you missed it, when you use a cell phone, never hold it against your head. Use speakerphone or SMS. I only use my phone when I have no other choice.

Reduce your body load from metal in the mouth: Talk to a holistic dentist about removing any mercury fillings (a neurotoxin, that may cross the blood-brain barrier). The same goes for other metal fillings, implants and pegs used in the mouth. Metal actracts EMF's.

Near Infrared Sauna – great for detoxing heavy metals (you can buy them but here's a link to some information on how to build one yourself)
http://drlwilson.com/articles/sauna_therapy.htm

Stay hydrated, drink pure water, or as pure as possible. At least, use a carbon filter.

Learn about Flower Essences (I take Yarrow for EHS and Evening Primrose Oil for PTSD/childhood trauma) http://www.fesflowers.com/

Learn about Energy Medicine and simple healing practices you can do by yourself. Many people (myself included) strongly believe that Energy Medicine is the future of medicine.
https://www.amazon.com/Energy-Medicine-Donna-Eden/dp/1585420212

Learn about good Nutrition (try anything that resonates with you. I like Ayurveda's 5000-year-old diet and health principles best. They feel right for me).

Learn about the healing powers of essential oils (lavender is my favorite. I use it as a perfume, on my pillows, everywhere. Love the scent. And it calms the nervous system. Organic oils are best).

Grow your own vegetable garden (look into permaculture).

Spend time in nature.

Learn about herbal medicine and herbal tea health benefits.

Read self-help books or watch inspirational talks on YouTube on spirituality, staying in the present moment and healing (to do so, turn off Wi-Fi and hard-wire your computer. This is the first thing you must do. An Ethernet cable only costs a few dollars).

Book a Myofacial release session.

Find a good Osteopath (more gentle than a chiropractor).

Look into cranio-sacral therapy.

Learn Qigong (many great online YouTube channels. Occasionally I use the one below)
https://www.youtube.com/channel/UC27B9CCAY2wOurQWpATdfgA

Acupuncture/Acupressure/Reflexology is great for healing the nervous system.

Try EFT tapping for pain management and anxiety.

Pay attention to what you put on your skin. Your skin absorbs everything you put on it. So don't use chemical laden shampoos, soaps, perfumes, shower gels, hair dyes, deodorants etc. Your skin absorbs everything. Basically, if you can't eat it, don't put it on your skin. The Internet is full of DIY beauty product recipes made from natural ingredients. I make my own toothpaste, deodorant, and shampoo...it's easy and it works just fine.

Treat your illness as part of your journey; it is here to teach you something.

Treat your body with respect, love and compassion.

Get some sunshine on your skin. Contrary to popular belief we need the sun and most people are lacking in Vitamin D3. You can take the supplements, but there's no substitute for the real thing.

Check out Donna Eden's Daily Energy Routine (Energy Medicine via Prune Harris)
https://www.youtube.com/watch?v=nN2uq78Y2bE

An Ayurvedic warm Sesame Seed Oil massage for grounding is a wonderful way to start the day or prepare for a good night's sleep.
https://www.banyanbotanicals.com/info/ayurvedic-living/living-ayurveda/lifestyle/self-oil-massage/

Learn how to breathe correctly (diaphragmatic breathing)

Learn Pranayama breathing techniques (alternate nostril breathing calms the nervous system like nothing else).

Google 'Healing the Vagus Nerve'. This will open up an entire new perspective on healing.

Study 'The Microbiome' to see how important gut health is for healing (everything is linked!)

I honestly feel that the above tips are essential for everybody to learn, regardless of whether or not you have a health challenge. In any case, they are a great introduction to this/our never ending journey of learning and healing.

Look up 'Oil Pulling' – it's great for helping your body to detox.

Remember this: The higher you can raise your level of health, the less symptoms become or feel troublesome (meditation is great for this). That being said, symptoms are messengers to let you know something is wrong. They are there for a reason, to bring about avoidance of a cause. Or to bring about imminent change.

"It is simply no longer possible to believe much of the clinical research that is published, or to rely on the judgment of trusted physicians or authoritative medical guidelines. I take no pleasure in this conclusion, which I reached slowly and reluctantly over my two decades as an editor of The New England Journal of Medicine." - Dr. Marcia Angell, a physician and longtime Editor-in-Chief of the New England Medical Journal (NEMJ)

CONCLUSION

Congratulations on taking the first step! If you have read this far, by now you know that EHS is a condition that, for many people doesn't exist. Except that more and more people are getting sick, including some with prominent names. Having said that, EHS is, at the time of writing, not yet acknowledged as a 'real' illness

here in France. They do occasionally mention people with EHS on TV... but it is usually in a derogatory manner...
"This woman/man living in a cave/forest/caravan in the middle of nowhere is under the *impression* that she/he is *allergic* to the modern world...to Wi-Fi and cell towers..."

Leaving one with the sense that these poor people are somehow deluded. Trust me, nobody in their right mind would *choose* to live in this way, to live in a shielded caravan in the forest alone, cut off from the rest of the world, and their loved ones.

Wouldn't it be heaven if we could all live in Sweden, where there exists an entire village for people who are EHS. Where they build apartment blocks with special materials that block electromagnetic waves to accommodate electro-sensitivity. That being so, I've often wondered how an illness can be 'official' in one country and not another. Should there not be common medical criteria (globally) by which to diagnose an illness such as this? Are we not all sentient beings made of flesh and blood?

What's more, the mobile industry tells us there is nothing to worry about. At the same time they are not bothered about investigating the effects of EMF's on the human body. I know what you're thinking. That it's not humanly possible. You can't really have a situation whereby human life is deliberately endangered and the powerful multi-billion dollar corporations are trying to cover it up. Or can you?

Sadly, when faced with an organization as powerful as the telecommunications industry that has the media, certain scientists and politicians in their pocket, you are up against a monster that's far too big to slay. You can't beat it. But you don't have to support it either.

Alas, our education is nothing short of brainwashing. Science is corrupted. And truths are swept under the rug because it threatens the interests of a few select, powerful people and the corporations they hide behind. We live in a society that's constantly telling us how things should be. We are not taught to question, to think for ourselves and to think critically. To do so requires taking a risk. Much easier to stick our heads in the sand and go with the flow.

But it doesn't have to be this way. You now know what you are up against. You know what to do when EHS happens to you. You know how to protect your body as best you can. And you know how to protect the people you love. Please take this information, and run with it. I wish you Love, Health, Peace and Freedom from the Matrix ☺

FINAL THOUGHTS

In the beginning of this book I stated that I'm proud to be EHS. An ambitious statement to be sure. But for, me, this 'hypersensitivity' has proven to be the greatest journey of my life so far. Essentially, what I mean is that today, I'm at the stage of owning not just my electro-sensitivity, but also my sensitivity in general.

By thinking of EHS as a special gift, I found a way of 'giving back' by sharing insights and information I gathered along the way.
Admittedly, health-wise I still have good and bad days and it's taken me some time to get to this point. To stop thinking of myself as flawed, weak and broken. To yield. To accept myself just the way I am and to stop any attempts at being like other people, living like other people, and keeping up with the masses has proven to be the biggest breakthrough.

I used to think I was missing out on a 'normal' life by not being able to participate. Now I've come to know a new kind of normal, and I have to say I like it. There has been much to process over the past few years. It's too complicated to put it all into words right here, right now. But to sum it up, it kind of feels like a rediscovery of how things were meant to be, and I've come to know the following: Life was meant to be simpler. Slower. Cleaner. Healthier. That is our birthright. In order to go forward we need to go back to basics. And peel back layer after layer of superficiality and artifice... letting anything that no longer serves health or personal growth just fall away. Kind of like a rebirth.

Finally looking at EHS as a gift instead of a curse and/or reason to abstain from life feels like an epiphany. As more and more people become overwhelmed, over-stimulated, over-zapped and unwell by modern living, the world can do with a unique expertise and insight. High-time I come out of my shell. So here I am. Here we are. Let's ride these 'waves' all the way to a remote tropical beach, paradise. No mobile phones or Wi-Fi allowed. Care to dance?

"When you learn, teach, when you get, give." - Maya Angelou

HEALTH RESOURCES

The BioInitiative Report - (A report on the relationship between the electromagnetic fields associated with power lines, wireless devices and health, published online by scientists, health professionals and researchers in 2007).
https://www.bioinitiative.org/

Dr Belpomme's diagnostic criteria for EHS and Multiple Chemical Sensitivity:
https://drive.google.com/file/d/1VnfzSRzmB6loJykb7r-WM8ufOpuo24Wm/view

Swiss Shield Fabric for protection against electromagnetic radiation:
https://www.swiss-shield.ch/index.php?&L=1

EHS websites:
http://lessemf.com/
https://www.electricsense.com/

Find a fresh water spring near you: http://www.findaspring.com/

An introduction to Ayurvedic vata, pita, kapha doshas: https://www.banyanbotanicals.com/info/ayurvedic-living/learning-ayurveda/vata-pitta-and-kapha/

Book: Healing with Whole Foods: https://www.amazon.com/Healing-Whole-Foods-Traditions-Nutrition/dp/1556434308

Prune Harris demonstrated how to energy self-test what foods can be assimilated and metabolized by your body: https://www.youtube.com/watch?v=kHEc7LhYOtE

Terry Wahl's TedX 'Minding your Mitochondria' talk: https://www.youtube.com/watch?v=KLjgBLwH3Wc&vl=en

Dr L Wilson on Hair Mineral Analysis https://www.drlwilson.com/articles/HA INTRO.htm

Learn Mindfulness and Meditation techniques - a free online course: https://palousemindfulness.com/

Enemas: As without, so within. A clean colon is vital for healing. Here's some information on coffee enemas (not as scary as it sounds...life-changing, in fact). https://www.drlwilson.com/articles/COFFEE ENEMA.HTM

Book: 'Earthing, the Most Important Health Discovery Ever! https://www.amazon.com/Earthing-Most-Important-HealthDiscovery/dp/1591202833

Near Infrared Sauna – great for detoxing heavy metals (you can buy them but here's a link to some information on how to build one yourself) http://drlwilson.com/articles/sauna_therapy.htm

Flower Essences (I take Yarrow and Evening Primrose Oil) http://www.fesflowers.com/

Book: Learn about Energy Medicine and simple, first aid healing practices you can do for yourself. Energy Medicine really is the future of medicine https://www.amazon.com/Energy-Medicine-Donna-Eden/dp/1585420212

Learn Qigong (many great online YouTube channels. Occasionally I use the one below) https://www.youtube.com/channel/UC27B9CCAY2wOurQWpATdfgA

Donna Eden's Daily Energy Routine (via Prune Harris) https://www.youtube.com/watch?v=nN2uq78Y2bE

Ayurvedic warm Sesame Seed Oil massage for grounding
https://www.banyanbotanicals.com/info/ayurvedic-living/living-ayurveda/lifestyle/self-oil-massage/

ABOUT THE AUTHOR

Tanja Bulatovic is an Australian actor and writer. She has lived in Japan, the Balkans, Austria, and Australia. In 2009 she moved to the south of France, where she currently lives with her husband. Her passions include the healing arts, travel, self-sufficiency (i.e. freedom from the matrix), location independence, and all things French.

Her interest in natural health began several years ago when her life turned upside down in order to recover from chronic health issues. For lack of help from conventional medicine, she learned if she was to heal she had to help herself. Since then, she became an avid researcher, seeker of truth, prolific self-discoverer and advocate for holistic healing methods, and her life has transformed in a big way. The experience of her crashing health woke her up and it continues to fuel all of her offerings as a writer, artist and human being.

Her mission is to inspire people to take control of their own health, and reverse disease with a radical transformation of diet and lifestyle. You can find her primary links and social media pages via the links below.

Web page: https://www.tanjabulatovic.com/

Twitter: https://twitter.com/tanjabulatovic

Facebook: https://www.facebook.com/TanjaBulatovicAuthor/

OTHER WORKS BY THE AUTHOR

Living in France Made Simple
French Men on Love and Women

PS. If you enjoyed this eBook and found it useful, please remember to leave a short review on Amazon. Reviews are vital Internet currency these days. On top of that, you'll be doing your bit to get the EHS/EMF message out in order to help other people. Thank you!

Printed in Poland
by Amazon Fulfillment
Poland Sp. z o.o., Wrocław